PARADOXES OF DEMOCRACY

Paradoxes of Democracy

Fragility, Continuity, and Change

S. N. Eisenstadt

THE WOODROW WILSON CENTER PRESS
WASHINGTON, D.C.

THE JOHNS HOPKINS UNIVERSITY PRESS
BALTIMORE AND LONDON

EDITORIAL OFFICES

The Woodrow Wilson Center Press
One Woodrow Wilson Plaza
1300 Pennsylvania Avenue, N.W.
Washington, D.C. 20004-3027
Telephone 202-691-4010
wwics.si.edu

ORDER FROM

The Johns Hopkins University Press
P.O. Box 50370
Baltimore, Maryland 21211
Telephone 1-800-537-5487
www.press.jhu.edu

2 4 6 8 9 7 5 3 1

Library of Congress Cataloging-in-Publication Data

Eisenstadt, S. N. (Shmuel Noah), 1923–
    Paradoxes of democracy : fragility, continuity, and change /
Shmuel Noah Eisenstadt.
        p.   cm.
    Includes bibliographical references and index.
    ISBN 0-8018-6309-0 (cl. : alk. paper)
    1. Democracy.   I. Title.
JC423.E374   1999
321.8—dc21
                                                                99-35073
                                                                    CIP

ABOUT THE CENTER

The Center is the living memorial of the United States of America to the nation's twenty-eighth president, Woodrow Wilson. Congress established the

Woodrow Wilson Center in 1968 as an international institute for advanced study, "symbolizing and strengthening the fruitful relationship between the world of learning and the world of public affairs." The Center opened in 1970 under its own board of trustees.

In all its activities the Woodrow Wilson Center is a nonprofit, nonpartisan organization, supported financially by annual appropriations from the Congress, and by the contributions of foundations, corporations, and individuals. Conclusions or opinions expressed in Center publications and programs are those of the authors and speakers and do not necessarily reflect the views of the Center staff, fellows, trustees, advisory groups, or any individuals or organizations that provide financial support to the Center.

To Marty,
master explorer of democracy,
friend of a lifetime

CONTENTS

PREFACE

The research presented in this book was started long ago—in 1988 when I was a Fellow at the Russell Sage Foundation. Since then, I have continued to work on the problems of democracy, attempting to bring my analysis within the framework of comparative studies of civilizations. This work has constituted the major focus of my research for the last two decades.

The final text of this book was prepared while I was a Fellow at the Woodrow Wilson International Center for Scholars in Washington, D.C., in the fall of 1996. In the meantime I have also conducted many seminars on the problems of democracy at the Hebrew University of Jerusalem, together with Professor Ruth Gavison.

Throughout the years I have discussed my research and related topics with Seymour Martin Lipset, to whom this book is dedicated, and Larry Diamond, as well as with Bjorn Wittrock and Dietrich Rushmeyer, when I was a Fellow at the Swedish Collegium for Advanced Social Studies in Uppsala.

Luis Roniger, Ruth Gavison, and Mark Warren have commented on earlier drafts of this book, and I am also indebted to two anonymous readers from the Woodrow Wilson Press for their very useful comments, and to Joseph Brinley, the director of the press, and Carol Belkin Walker, editor at the press, for their comments and encouragement, and to Ann Hofstra Grogg for her wonderful editorial work.

Last, I would like to thank my secretary in Jerusalem, Batia Slonim, for continual help; Marjo Schejtman, who provided research assistance, above all in the arduous preparation of the bibliography; Esther Rosenfeld in Jerusalem, who has faithfully typed and retyped the many—too many—drafts of this manuscript; and Doreen Unzeitig at the Max-Weber-Kolleg at the University of Erfurt, who typed the last versions thereof.

This work was supported by grants from the Israel Science Foundation and from the Chiang-Ching-Kuo Foundation.

PARADOXES
OF DEMOCRACY

INTRODUCTION

THE PROBLEM

I

Time is now ripe for a reappraisal of theories on constitutional democratic regimes. A great variety of recent experiences bear on their development and viability and seem, at least at first glance, to call into question some accepted assumptions about the conditions that support these regimes.

The general as well as the more scholarly discourse on democracy has long been guided by two contradictory assumptions. On the one hand it has been assumed that there is a natural human predisposition to democracy, an assumption increasingly prevalent and popular following the breakup of the Soviet regime and many authoritarian regimes in Southern Europe and Latin America. On the other hand, it has been assumed, from their very inception, that democratic regimes were aware of their fragility. This awareness was built, to some degree, on the political discourse of antiquity, but it was rooted above all in the direct experience of the modern era. The continuous threats constitutional democratic regimes have faced—from totalitarianism, communism, fascism, and national socialism—have haunted contemporary Western political discourse. Memories of the period between the two world wars, in particular, influenced the far-ranging literature on the preconditions of democracy and on the impeding crises thereof. Concerns for the viability of the state and for capitalism burgeoned in the social

1

sciences following the Second World War and on to the 1950s and early 1960s. At the same time the notion of the constitutional democratic regimes was reinforced by the breakup of many Third World democracies. India, and to some degree Sri Lanka, were the exceptions.

This continuous emphasis on impeding crisis did not take into account that in the West no democratic regime had collapsed since the end of the Second World War or that, indeed, at least in the West, the general trend seemed to go in the other direction, as authoritarian regimes—in Spain, Portugal, Greece, and lately even in some Latin American countries— became democratic. Neither did the "crisis" literature take sufficiently into account the fact that several non-European countries—notably India, Japan, and Israel—have been able to maintain constitutional democratic regimes since the end of the Second World War, as also have Germany and Italy, the two countries in which the breakdown of democracy in the inter-war period was most dramatic.

Only recently, from about the mid-1970s on, has the problem of transition to democracy—and not the breakdown of democracy—become a central focus of research.[1] This research has now begun to confront the earlier one on the potential crises of democracy. Accordingly, a reappraisal of the various theories of the conditions of constitutional democratic regimes should take into account the major reasons for their inherent fragility and their potential viability.

2

In most of the vast, rich scholarly literature, the major emphasis has been on broad social, economic, or cultural conditions that are conducive to the development of constitutional democratic regimes, or to their consolidation and continuity.[2] In this book I will focus first on another dimension of these regimes that is of central importance for understanding their fragility or continuity—namely, the tensions or contradictions inherent in their very constitution, in their basic premises, and in the basic characteristics of the political process that developed within them.

But while fragility is indeed inherent in the constitution and development of constitutional democratic regimes, at the same time these regimes exhibit a very high level of continuity and flexibility in the face of great social, economic, and ideological changes. Hence it is of central importance to analyze the roots and conditions of both their weaknesses and their strengths. That is the aim of this book. Accordingly, the plan of the book is as follows.

In the first chapter I shall analyze how fragility and instability are inherent in the very constitution of modern constitutional democratic regimes. I shall show how fragility and instability are rooted first in tensions among their basic premises and especially between the constitutional and the participatory premises, each with different and often contradictory ideological and institutional implications.

In the second chapter I shall analyze the roots of these different conceptions in the cultural and political programs of modernity. In the following two chapters I shall analyze those aspects of modernity that are especially important for understanding the problems of constitutional democratic regimes. Thus the third chapter focuses on the basic antinomies and tensions in the cultural program of modernity and the fourth chapter on the tensions between pluralistic and Jacobin tendencies in the political programs of modernity.

In the fifth chapter I shall analyze how these tensions are articulated in the political process of modern societies—above all in the major protest movements that develop within them. I shall indicate that it is the very openness of the political process in these regimes, and in their tendency to continually redefine the realm of the political, that explains their potential fragility.

In the sixth chapter I shall show that while the nature and orientations of such protest movements vary greatly among modern societies, yet they constitute a basic and continual component of the political process in all modern regimes, and especially in democratic regimes, in which they are a continual challenge to continuity.

In the seventh chapter I shall proceed from analyzing the conditions that contribute to the potential fragility of the constitutional democratic regimes to those which may assure their continuity and adaptability. The core of this analysis will be to assert that it is their openness, again, that provides for their continuity. In essence, democratic political processes make possible the incorporation, in basic, institutional frameworks, of the symbols, themes, and demands of protest movements. The openness of the modern political process may, in fact, give rise to the development of a non-zero-sum conception of the political "game." This conception makes it possible for political actors to give up the positions of power they enjoy at any given period and to consider acceding to the demands of other political actors or movements of protest.

Accordingly, in the eighth chapter I shall analyze the conditions under which the conception of politics as a non-zero-sum game tends to develop. Here I shall emphasize, in addition to such conditions of democracy as economic development and the rise of middle and organized working classes—all amply analyzed in the literature—the crucial importance of trust among different sectors of society and between such sectors and the centers of society. Then I shall analyze the importance of several variables in the constitution and development of trust that have not been given enough attention in the literature, especially the construction of different types of collective identity. In the last chapter I present some reflections on the vicissitudes of democracy in the contemporary scene.

Let us now proceed to the analysis of the basic premises of constitutional democratic regimes, the basic conceptions of democracy that developed within them, and the tensions between them, with their institutional repercussions.

CHAPTER ONE

CONSTITUTIONAL AND PARTICIPATORY CONCEPTIONS OF DEMOCRACY

I

The two most important conceptions of democracy inherent in constitutional democratic regimes from their beginnings are the constitutional and the participatory. These conceptions have characterized these regimes, being built into their premises and guiding their internal dynamics as well as informing the political and philosophical discourse that developed within them. These conceptions are complementary but also competing, and even to some extent contradictory.

In the last half century or so, the constitutional conception of democracy has been most clearly promulgated by Joseph Schumpeter[1] or at least closely connected with his name. In this conception, democracy is characterized by a continuous competition among different political leaders or entrepreneurs, by the possibility, as Karl Popper has put it, to throw out "bad" rulers,[2] or, as John Plamenatz has put it, by a free competition for power.[3] This competition assures the possibility of continuous changes of rulers, a possibility that is contingent on adherence to constitutional arrangements and rules.

Change of rulers is effected by means of elections that in most modern constitutional regimes—in contrast to the city-states of antiquity—do not entail the direct election of the rulers themselves but rather of some type of representatives, members of electoral colleges, parliaments, and the like, who then choose or confirm the government. It is indeed the representative institutions that constitute the core of modern constitutional democratic regimes, even if, as in presidential regimes, they are supplemented by direct elections of the executive, and in other regimes also by referenda.

These various constitutional arrangements for the election of rulers, the institutionalization of the responsibility of the executive to other, especially representative, institutions or directly to the electorate, and the ideology of the separation of powers and of mutual checks and balances among them constitute the fullest institutional manifestation of the idea of accountability of rulers. This idea has been central to the Axial civilizations, of which the European civilization, in which (and in one of its offshoots the United States) the first constitutional regimes developed, was one.

This definition of democracy emphasizes strongly the crucial importance of such constitutional arrangements and rules and of adherence to them as a—possibly *the*—core element of democratic regimes, as basic prerequisites for their functioning and continuity. One of the major functions of these constitutional arrangements, which have been promulgated and institutionalized in all modern democratic regimes, is to assure the possibility that would-be rulers compete in some established ways, according to some clear rules of the games. Adherence to these constitutional arrangements and rules assures the possibility that the losers of today may become the winners of tomorrow and that new groups of contenders may rise and are given a chance to compete. Such adherence also assures that the possibility of changing rulers is not just a onetime event, but is continuous. Such assurance necessitates, of course, the existence of major institutional arrangements such as freedom of association, of speech, and of communication, freedom from arbitrary arrest, and the like, as well as the existence of various independent, "intermediary"—public but not governmental—associations in which these arrangements are continually upheld. In the pure constitutional conception of democracy, these institutional arrangements are conceived mainly as very important conditions that assure the possibility of the continuity of such regimes. This conception of democracy does not belittle the importance of continual political activity by citizens in different associations, but neither does it see these activities as the central core of democracy. In the constitutional conceptions of democracy, such activities are conceived above all as conditions contributing to the smooth functioning of the constitutional democratic process.

Concomitantly, this conception of democracy, even if it recognizes the fact that modern constitutional democratic regimes developed historically in close relation to the liberal conceptions of the individual and of freedom, does not necessarily equate democracy with any specific values. It is only lately, on the contemporary scene, that these conceptions of democracy have been equated by some groups with extreme liberal, "libertarian" values and with an ideological semisanctification of a free-market economy.

2

The second conception of democracy can be designated as participatory. Following classical Greek usage, it defines democracy as government by the many—not by single rulers or by small oligarchies—and emphasizes that democracy can be effected only through the active, possibly continual participation of large sectors of the population in the political process. The "many" are all the citizens, however citizenship is defined.

Two major versions of this conception of democracy can be distinguished—the republican and the communitarian or "communal" (the term "communitarian" is used here in the generic sense, not in the sense of the contemporary debate between "liberals" and "communitarians"). Their common denominator is a very strong emphasis on the active participation of citizens in the process of governance. What that participation entails, however, differs greatly between the republican and the communitarian versions.

The republican participatory conception of democracy emphasizes above all the importance of responsible citizenship—the responsible participation of citizens, however limited citizenship may be, according to the existing rules of the game, in political deliberation and in the political process.[4] In this version, participation is manifest above all in continuous deliberations about the issues facing the body politic, especially about the public good, and is conceived as the performance, by the citizens, of their duties to the community.

In contrast, the various communitarian conceptions of participatory democracy view participation as the basic right of the members of the society. According to these views, it is participation, in as many arenas of social life as possible, that assures those taking part are able to control the conditions governing their lives through deliberation about and implementation of various policies.[5]

The communitarian versions of the participatory conception of democracy also emphasize the importance of including all members of a community—without limitations of property, qualifications, class, color, religion, ethnicity, gender, and the like—in the political community and their continual participation in the political process. Here participation is seen as the legitimate bearer of visions of the common good and even *as* the common good. Moreover, participation is envisaged to be important not only in the central political arena but also in other arenas, especially on the local level, such as in the workplace. Indeed, given the recognition that full participation on the central level is, in modern societies, necessarily limited, communitarians of different persuasions have continually emphasized the importance of extending the democratic process to many "micro"-level, local, or functional situations and as including a variety of associational activities. Some communitarians see citizen participation as more important than the continual functioning of the major representative institutions and of the electoral process. At the same time there often develops among communitarians, as we shall see, a strong ambivalence about the activities of intermediate institutions.

3

Each of these conceptions of constitutional democracy entails specific—and to some extent contradictory—institutional and ideological consequences and different attitudes to the basic institutional arrangements of constitutional democratic regimes. At issue are different attitudes about the rules of the political game and above all toward representative institutions, different conceptions of the bases of legitimacy, and different ideas about the relations between state and society. Above all, the two conceptions of democracy differ with respect to their emphasis on two basic values that have been closely related to the development of democracy—liberty and equality.

In constitutional conceptions of democracy, the basic institutions and constitutional rules are seen as the central core, even as the essence, of such regimes. The attitudes of the different participatory conceptions of democracy to the basic constitutional and institutional arrangements of constitutional regimes differ greatly—both from Schumpeterian or Popperian ones and from each other—in keeping with their different views of political participation.

In the republican version, such institutions, and the rules of the game prevalent in them, have been usually accepted as part of the way of life and civil tradition of the community.[6] Communitarian participatory conceptions of democracy tended on the whole to be more suspicious of the rules of the game, of the representative institutions, and of the various intermediary associations as the core of the democratic regimes and processes. It is here that the ambivalent attitude of the bearers of these conceptions to intermediate institutions and to constitutional rules can be seen. On the one hand, given the strong emphasis on the importance of participation on any level of social activity, the promulgators of these conceptions tend to be favorably disposed to such associations. But on the other hand, given their emphasis on immediate, direct participation, they can also be very suspicious of the formal aspects of these associations and see them as representing only partial interests. Even among the milder versions of communitarian participatory democracy, which accept the necessity and legitimacy of the representative and various intermediary institutions or associations, neither such institutions nor the rules of the constitutional democratic game have been conceived as constituting the central core of these regimes.

Indeed, the more extreme among those who hold the communitarian participatory conception have often perceived the electoral (and sometimes even the juridical) process as no more than a sham, a perversion of the true spirit of democracy, of full democratic participation, or of the attainment of social justice. Many communitarians have proclaimed that a just society can be achieved only through full democratic participation. Extreme versions of this conception have often claimed that formal constitutional arrangements, especially the representative institutions, cannot express the will of the people, the common will—for by their very nature they tend to represent the narrow egoistical interests of certain individuals and groups, above all those that are strong and wealthy. The most extreme participatory views have often totally negated the validity of these institutions, and even of participation in them, characterizing them as tending toward totalism and totalitarian democracy.[7] It is only lately in the contemporary debates, especially in the United States, that the advocates of communitarianism have upheld very strongly the importance of participation both in various intermediary associations and in the representative—local and national—institutions.

4

These different conceptions of democracy have been also closely related to the different modes of legitimation of constitutional and democratic politics—on the one hand legitimation in terms of rules of the game, and on the other hand legitimation in different substantive terms.

The attitude of many promulgators of the constitutional (Schumpeterian) conception of democracy to any substantive aims of democracy is on the face of it rather skeptical or at the best neutral. In this conception constitutional democracy is legitimized by adherence to the rules of the constitutional game. The adherence to such rules is to some extent defined in terms of civility—that is, the acceptance of the existing norms and customs of the society and adherence to them, seemingly without looking for any further aims of democracy.

Yet implicitly at least, this emphasis on upholding the various rules of the democratic game seems meaningless without reference to some values, to some legitimation of constitutional democracy beyond the rules themselves. Historically this conception of constitutional democracy was very close to the development of liberalism, especially to the emphasis on the rights of individuals as antecedent to the constitution of society. Thus, paradoxically enough, even the constitutional conception of democracy, which strongly emphasizes adherence to the rules of the games, often justifies such adherence in terms of some basic conceptions of freedom, of "negative" liberty, of unalienable individual rights, and the like, thus illustrating that very often the legitimation of these regimes is also related to, or based on, upholding some substantive visions of overall political programs. Such visions may very often be couched—to follow Edward Shils—in primordial or sacred terms as well as civil terms.[8]

A closer look at the different conceptions of democracy indicates that there exists an elective affinity between them and the different bases of legitimation of democratic regimes. Communitarian conceptions show a very strong elective affinity to some combination of primordial and/or sacred legitimation of democracy, while constitutional republican conceptions show a very strong affinity to legitimation of democracy in civil terms. In this civil conception there may also develop an emphasis on the overall ways of life of the community that can contain primordial elements. While the relative importance of these different bases or components of legitimation vary greatly among different constitutional democratic regimes and in different periods of their history, these bases are inherent in these regimes, and in all these regimes there developed some combinations of and continuous potential tensions between them.

5

The different conceptions of democracy also denote different attitudes to the relations between the state and civil society, to their relative priority or hegemony, to the proper scope of the activities of the state, and to the tensions or potential contradictions between liberty and equality—two basic premises of these regimes.

The modern constitutional regimes crystallized, as we shall see in greater detail later, against the background of the development of the nuclei of highly autonomous civil society, of large sectors of society that were no longer embedded in traditional ascriptive units or regulated by the state but which, at the same time, had some at least potential access to the political center. Since then, the problem of the relations and the tensions between state and civil society has constituted a central aspect of the development of modern constitutional regimes.

The constitutional conception of democracy tended on the whole to emphasize the autonomy of civil society as against the state, while the participatory, and especially the communitarian conceptions of democracy could often imply a tendency to conflate the state and civil society. It is only lately that there developed among the recent advocates of communitarianism, as promulgated especially in the United States, a strong emphasis on the autonomy of civil society. Under appropriate conditions such conflation could give rise to the predominance of the state (or of a Jacobin party) over civil society.

These attitudes to the state and civil society were closely related to different emphases on liberty or equality. Both liberty and equality constituted basic components of the cultural program of modernity, of the very nature of constitutional and democratic regimes, and of the political community as a self-constructing and self-reflexive entity. But at the same time there could develop, as has been so often stressed in the literature, far-reaching tensions and contradictions between them. Constitutional conceptions of democracy have strongly emphasized liberty, as well as the legitimation of multiple interests, as at least one of the components or bases of constitutional democratic regimes. For the various communitarian participatory conceptions of democracy, equality—whether of responsible citizens, of members of the overall social community, of the local community, or of the community of the workplace—has been predominant.

6

Closely related to the different attitudes to representative institutions, to the rules of the political constitutional game, and to associational activity as promulgated by the bearers of the different conceptions of democracy have been different attitudes to the proper scope of the activities of the state.

The conception of democracy as a free and continuous competition for power, or as the possibility to throw out bad rulers, in principle favors a relatively limited scope of state or governmental activity. The emphasis on constitutional arrangements and rules of the game attests to a potentially deep distrust of concentration of power that characterizes these regimes. This distrust is manifest in the ideology and practice of the separation of powers among the different organs of government, especially the judiciary, the legislative, and the executive, in the system of mutual checks and balances among them, and in the independence of the judiciary. All these arrangements were first fully embodied in the United States Constitution, but they are also, in different yet concrete ways, found in other constitutional democracies. This distrust of the state has roots in classical liberalism of the seventeenth through the nineteenth centuries and in the long struggles of modern constitutional regimes against absolutist rulers. The promulgators of this conception of democracy looked with great suspicion on the extension of the powers of the state, seeing it as a possible threat to liberty and to a continuous free competition for power. It is no accident that Schumpeter, who predicted what to him seemed the inevitable extension of such powers through the victory of socialism, was also very skeptical about the future of democracy.

The republican version of the participatory conception of democracy is somewhat neutral on this matter, although many of its exponents tend to be suspicious of too wide a scope of governmental activities, especially of far-reaching regulation of private property that could undermine the existence of a free citizenship. If, however, for the classical liberals various rights such as liberty and private property were seen as rooted in basic natural rights and constituted a basis for the legitimation of constitutional regimes, in the republican version private property was seen more as a condition that enables citizens to exercise their civic duties without having to worry too much about economic matters.

The participatory conceptions of democracy, especially its communitarian versions, entail a different attitude to the extension of the scope of state activities, one that is basically or at least potentially very positive. The state—or other organs of the community—are seen in principle not only as very important agencies for the provision of many basic services to the community but also as among the more important instruments for changing conditions, especially great inequalities, that are detrimental to the proper functioning of democracy and that deplete its real meaning.

Various versions of participatory democracy often claim that only the activities of the state or of other collective agencies can mitigate the marked inequalities in power or wealth that develop in modern capitalist societies and make the free competition for power and the possibility of real political participation a farce. According to such views, only the mitigation of inequality will enable the exercise, by wider sectors of the society, of those basic natural rights that constitute the core of the liberal, democratic regimes. These attitudes explain the transformation of concrete conceptions of liberalism on the contemporary American scene. The strong predisposition, among many groups that designate themselves as liberals from the New Deal on, to advocate wide-ranging state actions in the social and economic arenas, has been rooted in their belief that only through such actions can conditions of economic inequality, which are inimical to the working of a democratic system, be changed. Moreover, in many of the participatory conceptions of democracy the state—or other collective agency, like a hegemonic party—is seen as the embodiment of some overarching vision that epitomizes the common will of society.

This positive attitude of communitarians to the activities of the state is closely related to their ambivalence regarding representative institutions and even intermediary associations and to their suspicion that these institutions may both impede the full participation of citizens in the political process as well as serve to perpetuate the existing, unequal distribution of power and wealth.[9]

The various attitudes to representative institutions, to the rules of the game, to various intermediary associations, to the relations between state and society, and to different modes of legitimation of these regimes touch on one of the most complex issues in democratic theory and practice. This is the problem of the relations between, on the one hand, the assurance of some seemingly unalienable rights—such as freedom of speech, of association, of information, and the like—and, on the other hand, the basic corollary to the rules of the constitutional game, namely the acceptance of the verdict of the majority, of majoritarian decisions. Can the decisions of the majority, democratically arrived at, abolish or override such seemingly unalienable rights, or do these rights stand as basic limits to majoritarian decisions?

These various conceptions of democracy were inherent in the constitution and development of constitutional democratic regimes, and we shall proceed now to the analysis of their historical roots.

CHAPTER TWO

THE HISTORICAL ROOTS OF CONSTITUTIONAL DEMOCRATIC REGIMES

I

These different conceptions of democracy, with their institutional repercussions, are not just academic or the exercises of scholars and intellectuals. They are rooted in the historical background of modern states and in their modern cultural and political programs. They were inherent in the formation and dynamics of modern constitutional democratic regimes, and they continue to constitute the foci of modern political discourse, process, and struggle.

Like all modern regimes, constitutional democratic regimes developed within the framework of the formation in Europe of modern territorial states and developed with the crystallization of new types of collectivities, with the evolution of new state-society relations most fully manifest in the emergence of civil society, with the concomitant transformation of political processes and, finally with the rise of modern market, capitalist, political economies.

The emergence of the first modern states in Europe entailed administrative centralization and relatively clearly defined territorial boundaries. The political community was conceived as autonomous, no longer subsumed under a broader "religious" canopy. This conception, which emerged in continental Europe and in England in close connection with the Reformation, Counter-Reformation, and the ensuing Wars of Religion, involved the transformation—even if haltingly and intermittently—of the basic conception of sovereignty that began as *dominium politicum and regale.*[1] In many continental states, the state was now defined in secular terms, even if absolutist kings claimed some type of divine legitimation—the so-called divine right of kings. It was the sovereign—the king or the state ("L'Etat c'est moi")—who was presented and promulgated, even if never wholly unchallenged, as the embodiment of what could be called the general will, the common good of society.

The representative institutions that anteceded the development of the modern state constituted a basic component of the institutional format of premodern European societies. They were rooted in some of the basic premises of European civilization briefly referred to above, above all in ideas about the accountability of rulers that were prevalent in Europe—accountability either to a higher law and/or to the community. Although these conceptions—derived both from tribal traditions and from republican ideas—weakened in many absolutist states, even if not in England or Holland or for a certain period in Sweden, yet they constituted at least the potential counterweight to absolutism and the major arena in which the political transformations mentioned above took place.

A further transformation of the basic concepts of sovereignty occurred, as we shall see later, with the Great Revolutions—the English Civil War or Great Rebellion, the American Revolution, and the French Revolutions. Secular definition of popular sovereignty gave rise to concomitant transformations of ideas about representation and citizenship.

The development of new, modern states and their legitimation were closely interwoven in European societies with the development of new types of collectivities—of collective identity or consciousness. The most important dimensions of this development were, first, the formulation of secular definitions, often in highly ideological terms, of the components of collective identity—civil, primordial, and universalistic, and transcendental or sacred;[2] second, whether religious or secular, the growing importance of the civil components; third, a continual tension among the different components; and fourth, a very strong emphasis on territorial boundaries as the main loci of the institutionalization of collective identity. The emphasis on the territorial components of collective identity and of political formations implied a very strong connection between the construction of states and that of the major, "encompassing" collectivities. Such construction entailed a congruence between the cultural and political identities of the population of the political territory; an emphasis on the primordial components of collective identity, as this component was reconstructed in some protonational ways in this period; and the promulgation of strong symbolic and affective commitments to the center of most sectors of society. This construction became epitomized in the tendency to the construction of what was to be called later, in the nineteenth and twentieth centuries, the nation-state.

2

The development in Europe of modern states and collectivities and the transformation of the notion of sovereignty were closely related to changes in the power structure of society, namely, the emergence of multiple centers of economic and political power and the development of some nuclei of distinctive new types of civil society and of public arenas or spheres.

The development of multiplicity of centers of power and of the nuclei of civil society was closely related to the development of a new type of political economy and of new modes of production, namely the market economy, first of commercial and later of industrial capitalism. In this period commercial and proto-industrial capitalist economies, market ideologies,[3] and a strong ideological emphasis on the rights to private property emerged. These processes created the nuclei of relatively independent centers of power that were potentially beyond the reach of the political (whether absolutist, republican, or revolutionary communitarian) powers. At the same time these new centers of power often claimed—in line with the older traditions of representative institutions in Europe—the right of autonomous access to the centers of power. Concomitantly there developed potentially autonomous public arenas. It was indeed the continual constructions of such public arenas, independent from both any single ascriptive sector and from the state, but possibly rooted in many such sectors and above all having an autonomous access to the central political arena, to the state, that constituted the epitome of the new type of civil society that developed in this period in Europe. In contrast to the earlier medieval period in which many disperse public spheres developed without necessarily confronting a relatively centralized state, in this period there developed tendency to the unification of such spheres and their continual confrontation with the centralized state.

The last—but certainly not least—of the processes crucial for the formation of modern European societies and political dynamics were those generated by the development of capitalist—first commercial, later on industrial capitalist—political economy.

The development of capitalist economies, of the international capitalist system and its concomitant continuous economic expansion, entailed the creation of new classes and new social strata—various new upper "capitalist" classes as well as industrial workers, the proletariat, giving rise to new types of class relations and confrontations. This development was closely connected with continual shifts in the distribution of resources and in the modes of access to them. Many sectors of society experienced social dislocation, and certain excluded social groups struggled for access to the central institutional frameworks and arenas.

All these institutional developments took place as the European state system emerged through political and military actions. In this state system, the mobilization of resources for war constituted a central component.[4] These developments also served as a springboard for political and military expansion beyond Europe, giving rise to colonial, imperial, and economic expansion throughout the world and the imposition of capitalism and modern political ideologies. This expansion spawned a tendency—rather new and practically unique in the history of mankind—to the development of universal, worldwide institutional and symbolic frameworks and systems. Several worldwide economic, political, and ideological systems emerged, all of them multicentered with continually shifting hegemonies within them and each generating its own dynamics and its own reactions to the others, with the interrelations among these frameworks and systems continually changing. Thus there was continual confrontation among the societies incorporated in the new international systems, above all between the various hegemonic (initially Western) centers and different peripheries and between the premises of the cultural program of modernity and the premises of non–Western European civilizations.

A crucial component of this confrontation was that, despite its universalistic premises, European expansion gave rise to very strong exclusivist tendencies.[5] These were closely related to the construction of a specific European self-conception in relation to other civilizations—a self-conception that entailed a distinct hierarchical ordering of different civilizations, with European civilization on the top.

All these institutional developments constituted not only the historical background of modern cultural and political programs but also the arenas in which these programs—with their inherent antinomial tensions and contradictions—were continually played out and institutionalized as they constantly confronted changing conditions.

CHAPTER THREE

THE CULTURAL AND POLITICAL PROGRAMS OF MODERNITY: BASIC PREMISES

I

It is against the background of these institutional processes and developments that modern cultural and political programs took shape. In them were rooted the ideological dimensions of the different conceptions of democracy.

Behind these programs loomed some very powerful, even if sometimes hidden, metanarratives of modernity. The most important among these were—following Edward Tiryakian's felicitous expression—the Christian, in the sense of affirmation of this world in terms of a higher, not fully realizable vision; the gnostic, which attempts to imbue the world with a deep hidden meaning; and the chthonic, which emphasizes the full acceptance of the given word and the vitality of its forces.[1] These different metanarratives were closely related to the different historical roots of the modern cultural program, especially as it crystallized in the Reformation and Counter-Reformation, the Enlightenment, and in the Great Revolutions.

The most important historical roots of the cultural and political programs were, first, the political theories of antiquity and the republican tradition as it developed in the Renaissance, Reformation, and Counter-Reformation. These theories promulgated the republican models of antiquity and the covenantal conceptions as they developed in the Reformation.

A second central ideological component of these programs goes back to, and in many ways incorporates, some of the basic premises of account-ability of rulers to some higher law—the Word of God or the Mandate of Heaven—that have been characteristic of the Axial age civilizations, of which Europe was, of course, one.[2] The third major ideological compo-nent of modern cultural and political programs was the emphasis on the autonomy of the individual and the closely related, if not identical, legiti-mation of private interests. This emphasis developed in concert with the ideology of individualism and was reinforced by the development of new economic forces of the market.[3] Fourth, there were the political traditions of representation referred to above. A fifth central ideological component of these programs was the utopian eschatological one, the search or quest for an ideal social order. The utopian visions that developed in these pro-grams entailed the transformation of Christian eschatology into a secular vision of the unfolding of human destiny.

In the Great Revolutions these various components were brought together and intensified. Through the interweaving of these ideological themes with the specific institutional processes described above, the mod-ern cultural and political programs, with their manifold institutional im-plications, common features, and internal tensions and contradictions, took shape.

The Great Revolutions constituted the culmination of the sectarian, het-erodox potentialities that developed in the Axial civilizations, especially in those in which the political arena was conceived as one means for imple-menting their transcendental vision. This transformation entailed turning upside down—even if ultimately in secular terms—the hegemony of the Augustinian vision, which promulgated the separation of the City of God from the City of Man and the concomitant attempt to implement hetero-dox visions, and sectarian visions, often imbued with strong gnostic ele-ments, that wanted to bring the City of God to the City of Man. The Great Revolutions can indeed be seen as the first or at least the most dramatic, and possibly the most successful, attempt in the history of mankind to im-plement on a macrosocietal scale utopian visions with strong gnostic com-ponents. It was, indeed, Eric Voegelin's great insight—even if he presented it in a rather exaggerated way—to point out these roots of the modern political program in the heterodox and gnostic traditions of medieval Europe.[4]

This program entailed a far-reaching transformation of the conception of the relations between the transcendental and the mundane orders and, concomitantly, of the basic conceptions of political realm, of authority, and of center-periphery relations. This program gave rise, perhaps for the first time in the history of humanity, to a belief that the transcendental and mundane orders could be bridged and that some of the utopian, eschatological visions could be realized in the mundane orders and in social life. Since then the search for the ways in which the concrete social order could become the embodiment of an ideal order became a central component of the modern political discourse and tradition, and it was closely connected with the charismatization of the center as the area in which such visions can and should be implemented, a process that fully crystallized in the Great Revolutions.

Accordingly, this program combined orientations of rebellion, protest, and intellectual antinomianism, together with strong orientations to center formation and institution building, and gave rise to movements of protest carried out by intellectual and political activists. The institutionalization of this program did not, however, obliterate the relative autonomy of its various components described above. On the contrary, this institutionalization gave rise to the development within this program of continual tensions between these components and their ideological and institutional implications. These later became manifest in the different conceptions of democracy.

2

The radical innovation of this cultural program, of this new tradition, even if it could be seen as a transformation of the premises of the preceding traditions, lay in several major, often conflicting, tendencies and premises. All these tendencies shared a strong common denominator: the change of the place of God in the construction of the cosmos and of man, and for the understanding of their nature and characteristics.

The most important components of this program were, first, the "naturalization" of man, society, and nature; second, the promulgation of the autonomy and potential supremacy of reason in the exploration and even shaping of the world; and third, the emphasis on the autonomy of man.

Man and nature tended to become naturalized, that is, tended to be increasingly perceived not as directly regulated by the will of God, as in the monotheistic civilizations, nor as regulated by some higher, transcendental metaphysical principles, as in Hinduism and Confucianism, nor as regulated by the universal logos, as in the Greek tradition. Rather, they were conceived as autonomous entities regulated by some internal laws that could be fully explored and grasped by human reason and inquiry. It was this naturalization of cosmos and of man that constituted the central turning point from the premodern to the modern cosmological and ontological vision.

These transformations in the basic conceptions of the relations among man, cosmos, and God, as they developed in early modern Europe, especially in different sectors of the Enlightenment, were not initially necessarily antireligious. Indeed, many of them had very strong religious roots, especially in the Reformation, the Counter-Reformation, and their repercussions. At first the place of God as the Creator of the Universe was not denied. Rather, His place was reformulated in relation to man, cosmos, and nature. God, insofar as He remained in the picture, was more and more conceived as the Creator of that Universe which has generated laws of its own, laws that can be fully grasped by human reason and inquiry.

The exploration of such laws became one of the major foci of the new tradition. At the same time it was increasingly assumed that exploration of these laws would lead to an unraveling of the mysteries of the universe and of human destiny.

Concomitantly, central to this cultural program was emphasis on the growing autonomy of man: his (or "hers," but in this program certainly "his") emancipation from the fetters of traditional political and cultural authority and the continuous expansion of the realm of personal and institutional freedom and activity. Such autonomy entailed two dimensions—first, reflexivity and exploration, and second, active construction, mastery of nature, and mastery of society.

This exploration was not purely passive or contemplative. Indeed, a very strong assumption of this modern cultural vision, or at least of large parts thereof, was that through exploration not only the understanding but even the mastery of the universe and of human destiny, and a concurrent expansion of human environment, could be attained by the conscious effort of man.

The exploration of nature and the search for potential mastery over it tended also, at least in some versions of this new tradition, especially in some sectors of the Enlightenment, to extend beyond technical and scientific spheres into the social sphere. Such a view led almost naturally to the view that an investigation of human nature and of society could yield knowledge applicable to the social sphere proper. Such application was rooted in the belief that information and knowledge were relevant to the management of the affairs of society and to the construction of the socio-political order.

The situation was more complicated with regard to the autonomy of man. Man's naturalization and autonomy were conceived, as Immanuel Kant has shown, in two contradicting directions.[5] On the one hand, man was also seen as subject to the laws of nature, which he himself could explore. On the other hand, he was characterized by moral autonomy—seemingly, at least, transcending these laws and preceding a strong critical orientation as a basic component of this order.

Out of the conjunctions of these different conceptions there developed, within the modern cultural program, the belief in the possibility of active formation by conscious human activity rooted in critical reflection of cultural aspects of social, cultural, and natural orders. Society itself had become an object of conscious human endeavor oriented to its reconstruction. Such reconstruction usually entailed the possibility of active participation of various social groups in the formation of a new social and cultural order, as well as a high level of commitment to such orders. This reconstruction was also often seen as a basic component of the possibility of extending an individual's mastery over his (or "her," but here above all "his") own destiny.

Such conscious effort could develop in two—sometimes complementary, sometimes conflicting—directions. One has been the "technocratic" direction, based on the assumption that those in the know, those who mastered the secrets and arcana of nature and of man, of human nature, could devise the appropriate institutional arrangements for the implementation of human good and the good society. The second direction promulgated attempts to reconstruct society usually in a very totalistic way according to a cognitive—usually scientific—moral or religious vision.[6]

At the same time, there developed in this program very strong universalistic orientations, seemingly negating in principle the importance and significance of any specific political or national boundaries but also attempting to define a new socio-political order with broad, yet relatively definitive, boundaries.

3

Within the framework of this new cultural program the specific political program of modernity developed. The new ontological conceptions promulgated in the cultural program of modernity necessarily transformed the basic parameters and premises of the political order, of its legitimation, and of the conceptions of accountability of rulers. They also transformed basic orientations to tradition and to authority, as well as the basic characteristics of centers and of center-periphery relations.

This new political program, in close relation to the cosmologies promulgated in the Great Revolutions and to the institutionalization of the new political regimes that followed in their wake, entailed a radical transformation of the very conception of politics. The political arena was perceived as a distinct, autonomous ontological entity. The roots of this idea can be found in the Renaissance and the Enlightenment. When combined with the premises of the Great Revolutions it gave rise to the hope that political action could bridge the gap between the transcendental and mundane orders and help realize utopian and eschatological visions in the social order. For the first time political action was guided by a distinctive utopian vision. As in the broader cultural program of modernity, this vision could be technocratic, cognitive, or religious. The latter entailed the view that the political community is a self-constitutive and self-reflective entity, that society may, especially through political actions, continuously reconstitute itself in a consciously reflexive way.

At the same time, in close relation to the utopian component in modern political life, far-reaching transformations rooted in the utopian imagery of the Great Revolutions took place in the symbolism and structure of modern political centers as compared with their predecessors in Europe or with the centers of other civilizations. The crux of this transformation was, first, the charismatization of the political centers as the bearers of the transcendental visions promulgated by the cultural program of modernity. Second, and in combination with the first, was the incorporation of themes and symbols of protest, which were central components of the transcendental vision that asserted the autonomy of man and of reason.[7]

In contrast with almost every previous civilization, themes and symbols of equality, participation, and social justice became not only elements of protest oriented against the existing center but also important components of political legitimation of the regimes and of orderly demands by the periphery on the center.[8] The possibility of transforming some of society's institutional premises according to transcendental visions, through the promulgation of protest in terms of such visions, was no longer considered to be illegitimate or at most a marginal aspect of the political process. These visions became central components of the modern project of emancipation of man—a project that sought to combine equality and liberty, justice and autonomy, solidarity and identity of modern political discourse and practice. The incorporation of such themes of protest by the center heralded the radical transformation of various sectarian utopian visions into central aspects of the political and cultural programs. Simultaneously, there developed continual tendencies to permeation of the peripheries by the centers and of the impingement of the peripheries on the centers, with a blurring of the distinctions between center and periphery.

4

The transformation of the basic premises of the social and political order became interwoven with a parallel transformation and institutionalization of the conceptions of sovereignty, of citizenship, of representative institutions, and of accountability of rulers. The transformation of these premises entailed, first of all, a radical transformation of the basic concepts of sovereignty. The core of this transformation, which took place above all in the Great Revolutions, was the transfer of the locus of sovereignty to "the people" and the related development of the concept of popular sovereignty. At the same time, the concepts and practices of citizenship, representation, and accountability of rulers were transformed. Citizenship was changed from an acclamatory or ratifying act into a participatory act; representation was transformed from virtual to actual.[9] This new ideology of citizenship entailed the continual expansion, through political struggle and protest, of the access to representation in the center to all citizens, to all sectors of society.

In addition, the accountability of rulers was institutionalized. As Michael Walzer has shown, one of the most important innovations of the English Civil War was the fact that the king was not simply killed, but that he was executed after having been tried before a court of law, even if he did not accept the legitimacy of the court.[10] This innovation not only implied that rulers were accountable to some higher law, that they ruled under some Mandate of Heaven—a conception to be found in most Axial civilizations—but also specified the institutional mechanisms through which the rulers could be called to account. The great institutional innovation here was the location of the supervision of rulers and the accountability of rulers in specific mundane "routine" political institutions rather than, as in the premodern Axial civilizations, in ad hoc outbursts in charismatic individuals or in extrapolitical institutions, such as the Church—all of which claimed to be the authentic carrier of the higher law.

Closely related was the transformation of representative and juridical institutions, which became the major arenas in which the sovereignty of the people and accountability of the rulers could be implemented.[11] The supervision of rulers became located in these institutions. Later this notion evolved into the basic constitutional democratic premise according to which rulers are continuously elected, and in this way continuously responsible to the people, or at least to the electorate.

The transformations of the ideas of sovereignty, citizenship, and representation entailed a continual confrontation and crosscutting or overlapping between three complementary and yet also potentially antagonistic conceptions of authority that could be distinguished in the prerevolutionary period, especially in France. These conceptions were, first, the absolutist one, which was promulgated by the central royal-bureaucratic center that attempted to present itself as the central locus of authority by virtue of its being the bearer of rational enlightenment. The second conception held that the representative institutions—in France the parliaments with their juridical bases—were the loci of sovereignty. The last conception placed sovereignty in public opinion, ultimately in the popular will.[12] With the institutionalization of the modern postrevolutionary regimes, these different conceptions of authority became fused in modern parliamentary and judiciary institutions. The tensions between them transferred into tensions between the premises of representative and republican institutions and those of revolutionary or national communal participation—a tension that was at the core of modern regimes and of the different conceptions of democracy.

The most important institutional roots of the modern constitutional democratic regimes were the representative institutions that developed in medieval Europe—the various councils, parliaments, and assemblies of estates, many of them building on traditions of tribal assemblies. The crucial series of events that triggered the institutional system of this program and of the modern constitutional states were the Great Revolutions.

5

Out of the transformation of center-periphery relations, of the shift in notions of accountability of rulers, and of the incorporation of the symbols

and demands of protest into the central symbols of society came a continual restructuring of center-periphery relations that has been the central
focus of political process and dynamics in modern societies. Such continual restructuring was rooted in the fact that it was in this period that autonomous sectors of society developed. First taking place in Europe, the
development of the concept of civil society was a central part of this process.[13] Relatively passive, apolitical sectors of society became politically active, promulgating not only the discrete interests of different groups but
also different and competing conceptions of the common good, or from
more active actors in various dispersed arenas to at least potential participants in the central political arena.

Accordingly, the various processes of structural change and dislocation
that continually took place in modern societies as a result of economic
changes—urbanization, changes in the process of communication, and the
like—have led not only to the promotion by different groups of various
concrete grievances and demands but also to a growing quest for participation in the broader social and political order and in the central arenas
thereof. This quest of the periphery or peripheries for participation in the
social, political, and cultural orders, for the incorporation of various
themes of protest into the center, and for the concomitant possible transformation of the center, was often guided by the various utopian visions
referred to above and put forward above all by the major social movements
that developed, as we shall see later, as an inherent component of the modern political process.

This history of modern politics has in many ways become that of the incorporation of the symbols—the various symbols of protest and the demands of protest movements—into the centers of their respective societies
and of the associated transformation of center-periphery relations and
continuous restructuring of the boundaries of civil society in relation to
the state.

THE CULTURAL PROGRAM OF MODERNITY: ANTINOMIES, TENSIONS, CONTRADICTIONS, AND CRITICISMS

I

The crystallization from the eighteenth century on of the cultural program of modernity, with its multiple and continually changing institutional implications, entailed many antinomies, tensions, and contradictions. These gave rise to one of the most intensive discourses and socio-political dynamics in the history of mankind. They are also the basis of the different conceptions of democracy.

The contradictions were in many ways rooted in the different metanarratives of modernity referred to above—the Christian, the gnostic, and the chthonic—as well as in antinomies that developed in the Axial civilizations, especially in the tension between the drive to implement the transcendental vision in the mundane world and recognition of the imperfectibility of man. In the cultural program of modernity these antinomies became radically transformed into tensions among differing interpretations of the autonomy and hegemony of man and of reason, and of the very possibility of grounding morality and the moral order in them.

The most important tensions were, first, between totalizing and more diversified or pluralistic conceptions of the major components of this program, especially of the very concept of reason and its place in human life and society; second, between reflexivity and autonomy on the one hand,

and active construction of nature and society on the other; third, among different evaluations of major dimensions of human experience; and fourth, between control and autonomy, between discipline and freedom.

The dichotomy between totalizing and pluralistic visions has focused on accepting the distinctiveness of different values and rationalities as against conflating the different rationalities in a totalistic way. This tension developed first of all with respect to the very concept of reason and its place in human society. It was manifest, for instance, as Stephen Toulmin has shown, in the difference between the pluralistic vision of Montaigne or Erasmus as against the totalizing vision of reason promulgated by Descartes.[1] Among the most important conflations of different rationalities have been those that attempted to subsume value-rationality (*Wertrationalität*) or substantive rationality under instrumental rationality (*Zweckrationalität*) in its technocratic mode, or under a totalizing moralistic utopian vision, or, as for instance in communist ideology, under some combinations of both.

This tension between totalizing and pluralistic conceptions of human existence and social life developed also with respect to the course of human history—of its being constructed either by some overarching visions guided by reason or by the "spirit" of different collectivities against the emphasis on multiplicity of paths. The utopian, eschatological conceptions inherent in the belief in the possibility of bridging the transcendental and the mundane orders entailed also some very specific ideas of time, especially as related to the course of human history. Among the most important of these conceptions, many of which have been rooted in Christian eschatology, but constituted also far-reaching transformations thereof, was first a vision of historical progress and of history as the process through which the cultural program of modernity, especially individual autonomy and emancipation, would be implemented. This progress was defined above all in terms of universalistic values of instrumental rationality—of reason, science, and technology. But however future oriented this program was, it also developed references to an imaginary human communal past. It had, as well, a strong evangelistic and chiliastic trend, which, together with its "this-worldly" orientations, generated within it the very strong impetus to expansion.[2]

As against such totalizing visions of history there developed those often romantic visions—perhaps best represented by Giambattista Vico and later by Johann Gottfried von Herder[3]—that emphasized the multiple paths of histories of different societies and the autonomy of emotions. In its more conservative view, which developed most strongly in Germany, it stressed the distinctiveness of primordial collectivities but shared with the new cultural program of modernity many of the strong utopian, semi-eschatological conceptions, even if not the idea of progress.[4] In many countries the individualist, anti-institutional romanticism was predominant, while it faded in Germany.

The second tension that developed within the cultural program of modernity was that between different conceptions of human autonomy and its relation to the constitution of society and of nature. Of special importance in this context was the tension between, on the one hand, reflexivity and critical exploration of man, society, and nature and, on the other hand, active construction or mastery of nature and of human activity and society, often in a technocratic, engineering way. The emphasis on active construction of society and mastery of nature could become closely connected with the tendency, often found in cognitive conceptions rooted in the Cartesian heritage, to emphasize the radical dichotomy between subject and object, and between man and nature, reinforcing that radical criticism of the cultural program of modernity which claimed that it necessarily entailed an alienation of man from nature and from society.

The third major tension that developed within the cultural program of modernity concerned the relative primacy of different dimensions of human existence. Of special importance in this context has been evaluation of the relative significance of autonomy and the predominance of reason as against the emotional and aesthetic dimension of human existence, often equated with various vital forces, as well as with so-called primordial components in the construction of collective identities. Closely related were tensions among different conceptions of the bases of human morality, especially whether morality can be grounded in universal principles based above all in reason, in instrumental rationality, or in the multiple rationalities and multiple concrete experiences of different human communities.

2

Cutting across these tensions in the cultural program of modernity there developed a strong continual tension between control and autonomy, between discipline and freedom. This tension has two basic roots. The first, most general one was that the institutionalization of any ontological vision by definition entails limitations through the exercise of social control on human creativity.[5] But beyond this general fact, and more central to the understanding of the dynamics of modernity, this tension has been rooted in the continual—even if continually changing—contradictions between the basic premises of the cultural program of modernity and the major institutional developments of modern societies, which were to some extent at least inherent in this program.

The first such contradiction has been that between the emphasis on human autonomy and the strong controls rooted in the institutionalization of the cultural program according to the technocratic and/or moral visionary conceptions. These restrictive dimensions were analyzed from different but complementary points of view by Norbert Elias and Michael Foucault.[6] Among the most important manifestations of this control dimension were the civilizing process that started, according to Elias, in the absolutist courts of Europe and later in the homogenizing tendencies of the modern states, especially the postrevolutionary nation-states and ideas of the meaning of being civilized as they developed in bourgeois society. This contradiction has been aptly defined by Cornelius Castoriadis as that between (technocratic) mastery and (human) autonomy.[7]

Closely related have been the contradictions of modernity so strongly emphasized by Max Weber.[8] Thus, the second such contradiction was that between the creative dimension inherent in the visions that produced modernity—the visions of the Renaissance, Reformation, Enlightenment, and the Great Revolutions and the flattening of these visions, the disenchantment implicit in the growing routinization of these visions and above all in the growing bureaucratization of the modern world.

Third was the contradiction, also stressed by Weber, between an overarching vision through which the modern world becomes meaningful and the fragmentation of such meaning generated by the autonomous development of different institutional arenas—the economic, the political, and the cultural. Fourth was the contradiction between the tendency to self-definition and the construction of autonomous political units, above all states and nation-states and the continual growth of international forces beyond the control of such seemingly autonomous self-constituted political units.

All these manifestations of the tension between control and autonomy were inherent, as Peter Wagner has shown,[9] in the continual social and cultural changes attendant on the development of modern societies. These tensions have existed from the very beginning of the promulgation of the cultural program of modernity. They constituted a continual component in the development and unfolding of this program, with their latest formulations to be found in the discourse of postmodernism.

3

These internal tensions and contradictions within the cultural and political programs of modernity became, in the cultural discourse that developed around them, closely connected with the more extreme radical, "external" criticisms thereof. These more radical criticisms, rooted in the various metanarratives of modernity mentioned above and in the premises and antinomies of the premodern Axial civilizations, denied the validity of the claims of the promulgators of this program to ground its premises, and their institutionalization, in transcendental, metaphysical principles and/or to see them as epitomes of human creativity. The central point of most of these criticisms was the denial of the possibility of the grounding of any social order and of morality, as well as of human creativity, in the basic premise of the cultural program of modernity, especially in the autonomy and presumed immanence of man and in the supremacy of reason. Closely related was the denial of the claims that institutional development of modernity was rooted in transcendental vision, that it could be seen as the implementation of such vision and/or of human creativity. These criticisms asserted that, contrary to such claims, the institutionalization of these programs denied human creativity, flattened human experience, and led to the erosion of moral order and of the moral and transcendental bases of society, to the alienation of man from nature and from society, and to the weakening of human will and creativity.

These radical criticisms could be undertaken from two opposite—yet in some ways also curiously complementary—points of view. The first was the religious or traditional one, which espoused the primacy of tradition and of religious authority over the claims of reason and human autonomy, emphasizing that only the former can be the bearer of transcendental visions. The other criticism came from those proclaiming that such primacy denies the autonomy of human will and creativity.

It was the connection between the external and internal criticisms of the cultural and political program of modernity, perhaps best epitomized in the works of Friedrich Nietzsche and in the references to him in the works of later scholars like Ernst Jünger or Martin Heidegger,[10] that gave rise to the most radical criticism of the cultural and political programs of modernity. These criticisms emphasized the repressive dimensions of modern social life as it emerged in the nineteenth century up to the interwar period of the twentieth century. Above all, they emphasized the suffocating materialism of bourgeois society that—as against the spiritual aspects of the aristocratic age or the free spirit of human creativity—undermined the spiritual, moral, and communal dimensions of social life. In many of these criticisms materialism was seen as embodied in technology, which was seemingly the tool of the destruction of the moral and communal fabric of society and often closely related to the disenchantment of the world, to the development of the Iron Cage. But with the passing of time, with the full institutionalization of modern industrial societies, the attitude to technology among many of the critics of the cultural program of modernity, especially among the so-called reactionary modernists—for instance, Ernst Jünger, Hans Freyer, Carl Schmitt, and Martin Heidegger—became more complicated.[11] They attempted to spiritualize technology, to endow it with a communal or religious spirit, to portray it as a great achievement of human will and creativity that was debased only in depraved bourgeois society.

It is the multiplicity of the starting points for the discourse of the modern cultural and political programs, and the metanarratives that influenced the radical criticisms of them, that explains how these programs could be accused of a directly opposite fault. Thus, as Mark Lilla has shown,[12] they could be accused, as by the romantics, of releasing an aggressive form of reason, or by Søren Kierkegaard, Friedrich Nietzsche, Arthur Schopenhauer, and, in a different way, Leo Strauss of subordinating reason to hedonistic drives.[13] Similarly some critics could accuse this program of denying, by virtue of its absolutization of reason, the place of the sacred in modern societies, while others, like Voegelin, would accuse it of endowing reason with absolute, sacral dimensions.[14] Similarly some critics would accuse it of depoliticizing authority, while others would accuse it of politicizing, in a Jacobin mode, all human relations. The development of such seemingly contradictory criticisms of this program grounded in the narratives of modernity attest to the central importance of these very antinomies as a continual component of the discourse of modernity. Indeed, the multiplicity of these starting points of the modern cultural and political programs signify that modernity was continually perceived, within wide sectors of modern societies, as being—to use Leszek Kolakowski's felicitous expression—an "endless trial."[15]

THE POLITICAL PROGRAM OF MODERNITY: TENSIONS BETWEEN PLURALISTIC AND JACOBIN TENDENCIES

I

These tensions and contradictions bore also on the political arena and became manifest in it. In the wake of the Enlightenment and the Great Revolutions, the various ideological and institutional orientations and traditions analyzed in Chapter 4 came together in common cultural and institutional frameworks where they generated the tensions that have marked the political program of modernity and the political dynamics of modern regimes. These tensions have been greatly intensified by the charismatization of the center and the development of new center-periphery relations and new political processes in modern societies.

The first tension was between a constructivist approach—which views politics, especially democratic politics, as the process of reconstruction of society or, to follow Claude Lefort's or Johann Arnason's formulations, as active self-construction of society—as against a view that accepts society in its concrete continually changing composition. The second tension, closely related to the first, was between totalizing, often utopian and/or communal, visions—usually entailing a strong constructivist approach—and more pluralistic views. While pluralistic views do not necessarily deny a constructivistic approach to politics, they do entail the acceptance of society in its concrete yet continually reconstructed composition and of multiple patterns of life, of traditions, and of conceptions of social order that develop within it. This tension often coalesced with that between utopian and civil components in the construction of modern political arenas and processes, between "revolutionary" and "normal" politics.[1] Closely related was the third tension—that between the conceptions of politics as a totally autonomous dimension of human existence and will or existence as against seeing it as embedded in broader cultural patterns and social frameworks.

2

The central focus of these tensions as they crystallized in modern political discourse has been the relation between, on the one hand, the legitimacy of a multiplicity of discrete individual and group interests and of different conceptions of the common good and, on the other hand, of totalizing orientations that denied the legitimacy of the former and emphasized the totalistic reconstruction of society through political action.

On the ideological level, the development of pluralistic conceptions was historically connected with the growing concern in political thought, from the seventeenth century on, with the legitimacy of private interests and conceptions of the common good. This emphasis was rooted in, or connected with, theories of natural rights, especially the right to property. The attitude toward property changed from the republican view, which stressed its importance for freeing citizens for responsible participation in the political community, to the view that property embodied a "natural right," that it was almost a precondition of political community. Thus the political community became the guardian of property.[2]

This development was closely connected with a radical change in the concept and idea of the social contract. First of all, this idea as it developed in the modern period was based on the assumption—an assumption shared also by those who were opposed to the ideas of the social contract, like the romantics—that human nature constituted the social order and could not be superseded by any extrahuman element. Second, the modern idea of the social contract could—and often did—imply that the contract was connected with the establishment of a good, possibly ideal, order, an order understandable by reason and amenable to rational, even scientific investigation. It was from this point that the most radical difference from the conception of the social contract in the reflexive tradition of the Great Civilizations has emerged.

It would be wrong, however, to assume that the crux of the modern reformulation of the idea of the social contract was simply to legitimate the pursuit of individual, egoistic interests. Recognition of the legitimacy of private interests entailed also the legitimacy of plurality of interests and of different interpretations of the general will, or the common good.

The idea of social contract could be connected with rather different views of human nature and the best social order. It could be seen in John Locke, and later among the utilitarians, as the harbinger of political liberty. It could be used to justify, as in Thomas Hobbes, the construction of a modern Leviathan. Whatever their concrete political views, most of the modern contractualists searched for ways to connect individual rights with the establishment of a good, possibly ideal, social order that would realize the vision of reason and the good society.

Moreover, the modern reformulations of the social contract did not necessarily take for granted a natural harmony between individual interests and the good of society. Indeed, they recognized the potential tensions or even contradictions between the two.

The very assumptions guiding conceptions of the social contract exacerbated the problem of the relations between multiple interests and the common will or, to put it in Jean-Jacques Rousseau's formulation, of the relations between the "general will" and the "will of all."[3] Recognition of this problem constituted a central focus of modern political discourse. In modern societies the problem was made more acute by transformations of the ideas about representation and citizenship. These made popular sovereignty the locus of the general will or the common good of society, but at the same time they sharpened debate about the location of the general will and the relations between the general will and the discrete interests of individuals and groups.

Most participants in this discourse were concerned with the conditions necessary for the development of responsible citizenry. Individuals were perceived not only as egoistical, hedonistic, and utilitarian beings but also as potentially politically responsible citizens who may be also carriers of broader visions and upholders of civility. This concern could be found, as John Dunn has shown,[4] in Locke's emphasis on trust as the basic precondition of human society (curiously reminiscent of Emile Durkheim's conception of precontractual elements and solidarity), in the numerous discussions in *The Federalist Papers*, or in J. S. Mill's interest in education. Only in some of the more extreme formulations of the utilitarian and, recently, of the rational choice approaches was this concern given up. It was indeed in the work of Rousseau that the concern was most sharply confronted and fully articulated, especially in his analysis of the limited possibility of a balance between the egoistical will of all and the common will of society and in the opposition between the republican political idea of full participation of citizens in the body politic and the individualistic conception of man as a voluntary member of society.

3

The central dividing point in modern political discourse has been between the bearers of pluralistic conceptions that have accepted and even upheld the legitimacy of multiple private individual or groups' interests and of different conceptions of the common good, and those who denied it. Behind this division was a concern about the possible erosion among members of society, through the overemphasis on narrow individual or group interests, of commitment to the common good. This decreased commitment developed within pluralistic, democratic and antidemocratic, totalistic political traditions alike. Suspicion and preoccupation could be found, for instance, among the Founding Fathers of the American Revolution who promoted the constitutional conception of democracy and in the fear of factions expressed in *The Federalist Papers*. This fear has been even more pronounced among the promulgators of various communitarian participatory conceptions of democracy.

The concern about possible erosion of commitment to the common good was greatly reinforced by—indeed rooted in—the openness of the political process within modern regimes, most visible in their representative institutions, above all the parliamentary institutions (and to a smaller extent institutions of local government) and also the juridical ones. The representative institutions have continuously been the major arena in which different interests were promulgated and articulated, and so the fear that they would become forces of divisiveness in the body politic, undermining the common will, was very widespread in the modern political discourse, especially as political organizations devoted to the pursuance of such interests were most visible in the representative institutions.

But there developed a crucial difference with respect to these concerns as they evolved in constitutional pluralistic views as against the varieties of authoritarian, and above all totalistic or totalitarian, conceptions. The crux of this difference lay in the respective views espoused by the promoters of these different concepts about the possibility of development of responsible citizenry and leadership through an *open* political process. The promoters of the pluralistic conceptions of constitutional democracy were also fully aware of the possibilities of such erosion, but in their conceptions, the individual was recognized as a potentially responsible citizen and not simply as a purely egoistical, utilitarian, or hedonistic being. Accordingly in these conceptions the tendencies to erosion were seen as counteracted by active participation of citizens in the major institutional—especially political—arenas in which different interests and visions are transformed into policies articulating different visions of the common good. In contrast to the promoters of the authoritarian and totalitarian conceptions, promoters of the pluralistic conceptions searched for institutional arrangements that could assure the open expression both of different visions and of many discrete interests. According to them it was through such arrangements that the potentially open nature of modern political process and discourse, and the core characteristics of this process as the political self-reflection of society, can be continuously maintained.

The search for such institutional arrangements was manifest first of all in the promulgation of constitutions and in their implementation in the constitutional democratic regimes. Second, this search was manifest in the belief that the representative institutions, especially the parliamentary institutions, were the major arena in which the open nature of the political process was secured. Third, the search was manifest in the upholding of the rule of law and of the independence of the judiciary.

True, even in the authoritarian or totalitarian regimes, these premises were at least symbolically institutionalized and paid lip service to, but actual attitudes to them and their institutional dynamics differed greatly. In constitutional democratic conceptions, the emphasis on the constitutional, representative, and juridical institutions entailed the view that these were the arenas in which the search for some common good, for the institutionalization of the political collectivity as a moral community, could go hand in hand with the acceptance of existence of different conceptions of the common good and with representation, above all, of different interests through political parties. In contrast, the critics of democracy from the right and the left alike have often decried the inappropriateness of the parliamentary mode of political representation, wedded as it seems to be to the articulation of discrete interests and to the divisive aspects of the community, for putting forth the conceptions of the common good.[5] Within most of the authoritarian and Jacobin ideologies there developed a negative view of the representation in the parliamentary and juridical arenas of multiple interests and of multiple conceptions of the common good.

From religious and traditional camps through the various adherents of direct collective actions, like Georges Sorel, and of various populist conceptions up to outright totalitarianism, especially fascism on the right but also, in a different vein, the totalitarians on the left who advocate direct participatory democracy, the many critics of modernity have portrayed the representative institutions and to some extent also the juridical institutions, as basically demoralizing, as demeaning of any serious collective endeavor, as providing an arena either for the pursuit of narrow individual or group interests and/or for the display of baser instincts of the masses, and as inappropriate for the articulation of the general good, of the vision of the political as a moral community. They have looked for other institutional arrangements or arenas in which the divisiveness inherent in the very nature of democratic politics might be overcome.

While the number of candidates for such institutional arrangements has been large, the search has tended to two seemingly opposite, but sometimes also complementary, directions—the corporatist model and of totalitarian democracy. The corporatists generally eschewed democratic ideology and electoral practice and looked upon representative institutions as consultative bodies that could incorporate various legitimate interests under the canopy of a common good that would minimize their divisiveness. The other direction, that of totalitarian democracy, did not deny the representative institutions and open political process, but basically subverted them, as J. L. Talmon, R. Aron and Lefort have shown.[6] They attempted to construe these processes in ways that would remove all elements of openness and divisiveness, obliterating the dichotomy between discrete, special interests and generalized visions of the common good. The common denominator of the antipluralistic, authoritarian, and above all the totalitarian conceptions were various collectivistic orientations or ideologies that espoused the primacy of the collectivity or of collectivist visions.

Two such broad ideologies have been especially important in modern regimes. One emphasized the primacy of a collectivity based on common primordial and/or spiritual attributes—above all a national collectivity. The other ideology has been the Jacobin one. The essence of the Jacobin orientations, of Jacobin programs, has been the belief in the possibility of transforming society through totalistic political action. These orientations, the historical roots of which go back to medieval eschatological sources, developed fully in conjunction with the political program of modernity, and they epitomized the modern transformation of the sectarian attitudes to the antinomies of the Axial civilizations.

The Jacobin components of the modern political program have been manifest in a very strong emphasis on social and cultural activism, on the ability of man to reconstruct society by political action according to some transcendental visions. Closely connected is the very strong tendency to the absolutization of the major dimensions of human experience as well as of the major constituents or components of social order. Such Jacobin orientations tend to emphasize the belief in the primacy of politics and in the ability of politics to reconstitute society. Pristine Jacobin orientations and movements have been characterized by a strong predisposition to develop not only a totalistic world view but also all-encompassing totalitarian ideologies that promulgate a total reconstitution of the social and political order and espouse a strong—even if not always often universalistic—missionary zeal. These orientations have been manifest above all in attempts to reconstruct the centers of their respective societies, in the almost total conflation of center and periphery, negating the existence of intermediary institutions and of what has been often called civil society.

The Jacobin component has appeared in different concrete guises and in different combinations with other orientations and institutional tendencies. In its pristine modern forms, it developed first in leftist revolutionary movements, which often conflated the primacy of politics with the implementation of a technologic or moralistic vision of progress and reason. But the Jacobin component has been present, as Norberto Bobbio has emphasised,[7] not only in socialist but also in nationalistic and fascist movements, where it is closely interwoven with movements emphasizing the primacy of primordial communities. The Jacobin component is also strongly evident in many populist movements.[8] It is also closely interwoven with the upholding of the primacy of religious authority, as is the case in the contemporary fundamentalist movements. And it is manifest in more diffuse ways, as for instance in the intellectual pilgrimage to other societies, in attempts to find there the full flowering of the utopian revolutionary ideal,[9] and in many totalistic attitudes that flourish in various social movements and in popular culture. In all these settings, the Jacobin component has become connected to the different antinomies of modernity developed within them. On a more general level the homogenizing tendencies promulgated by most modern nation-states, especially those that emerged after the Great Revolutions, were strongly imbued by such Jacobin orientations.

Whatever the concrete manifestations of the Jacobin orientations, they constituted a continual component of the discourse of modernity. It is indeed the continual confrontation between the Jacobin component and orientation and the more pluralistic orientations, as well as among different Jacobin ideologies, that constitutes a central core of that discourse.

4

The contradiction between, on the one hand, the emphasis on an encompassing revolutionary or technocratic vision and, on the other hand, the acceptance and legitimation of the possibility of multiple views about political and social matters and the closely related emphasis on procedural rules that is of the essence of constitutional regimes, became fully visible in the Russian, Chinese, and Vietnamese revolutions. But its ingredients could be identified quite explicitly in the Jacobin groups and ideologies in the French Revolution and, more implicitly, in some Puritan groups, in England, the United States, the Netherlands, and in a more tortuous way in modern France. In all these societies the constitutional option, based on the recognition of the legitimacy of multiple interests that developed despite the revolutionary origins, won the day.[10] Indeed one of the most important problems in the analysis of modern constitutional democratic regimes is to understand how the recognition of the legitimacy of multiple views of the good society could develop from such revolutionary origins, with their monolithic totalistic visions.

5

These different conceptions of the relation between the individual and the social order generated some of the basic tensions in modern political discourse and its dynamics—namely, those between liberty and equality, between emphasis on a vision of the good social order and the narrow interests of different sectors of the society, between the conception of the individual as an autonomous sovereign and emphasis on the community, between the utopian and the procedural components of this program, and the closely related tensions between revolutionary and normal politics. In the political program of modernity, these tensions and antinomies coalesced above all in the form, to follow Hermann Luebe's terminology, of the tension between freedom and emancipation, which to some extent coincides also with Isaiah Berlin's distinction between negative and positive freedom.[11]

These various tensions in the political program of modernity were also closely related to those between the different modes of legitimation of modern regimes, especially but not only of constitutional and democratic polities. These were between, on the one hand, procedural legitimation in terms of civil adherence to rules of the game and, on the other hand, religious or secular-ideological components with a very strong tendency to promulgate other substantive modes or bases of legitimation—above all, to use Edward Shils's terminology, various primordial or sacred components.[12]

THE POLITICAL PROCESS IN MODERN SOCIETIES: PROTEST MOVEMENTS AND THE REDEFINITION OF THE POLITICAL

I

These basic tensions inherent in the political program of modernity—between visions of a better social order and recognition of discrete interests of individuals and subgroups, between liberty and equality—have been inherent in all modern, postrevolutionary regimes, be they authoritarian, totalitarian, or constitutional democratic. In the constitutional democratic regimes these tensions have become fully articulated in the different conceptions of democracy—the constitutional view and the different participatory views, and in their attitudes to basic institutional frameworks and to the bases of their legitimation.

These different conceptions of democracy have their roots in the historical processes through which modern political regimes have taken shape. The first, constitutional Schumpeterian definition, with all its ramifications, and the closely related pluralistic orientations, were to no small degree rooted in the heritage of representative institutions and practices as they developed in the early modern age.[1] The various participatory definitions of democracy grew out of attempts during the Renaissance and the Reformation to reconstruct the republican traditions of antiquity. Above all, the communitarian vision owes its origin to the many heterodox and intellectual movements of the late Middle Ages and early modernity, and especially of the Great Revolutions.[2] These different historical traditions have been continually transformed as the political program of modernity emerged, generating within it the tensions analyzed above—tensions that become fully articulated in the political arena in the different conceptions of democracy and in their ideological and institutional repercussions, also analyzed above. The confrontation between these different conceptions of democracy and their attitudes to the basic institutional frameworks of the modern constitutional regimes constituted the continual challenge to their continuity.

2

These different conceptions of democracy and their institutional derivatives were not unbridgeable. Indeed, in the more stable constitutional regimes there developed some combination between the major institutional implications of these different conceptions, giving rise to what Edward Shils calls civil society and which he distinguishes from both Schumpeterian "retrospective democracy" and from "mass society" (participatory democracy, in our discussion):

Liberal democracy is the most general class of society, variants of which, among others, are mass democracy, "retrospective" democracy and civil society. Mass or populist democracy is a variant of liberal democracy. It is at another pole from civil society insofar as it considers one stratum of society, albeit the majority of the population, as the properly sole beneficiary of policies regarding the distribution of goods, services and honours. Mass democracy would disregard representative institutions, replacing them by demonstrations and plebiscites. Mass democracy is conducive to demagogy and to the extension of governmental powers for the provision of substantive justice. Still, another alternative is the "retrospective" democracy formulated by Max Weber in his conversation with Ludendorff in 1919 and by Joseph Schumpeter in which the electorate confirms or dismisses its rulers in accordance with whether it is satisfied with their accomplishments during the most recent electoral period. Civil society differs from mass democracy in its concern for the interests and ideals of all sections of the population and not just for one. It differs from "retrospective" democracy in its constant scrutiny and assessment of government and its refusal to allow it to extend its range or depth of activities.[3]

A somewhat similar definition of democracy is given by Philippe Schmitter and Terry Karl:

> Modern political democracy is a system of governance in which rulers are held accountable for their actions in the public realm by citizens, acting indirectly through the competition and cooperation of their elected representatives.
>
> Modern democracy, in other words, offers a variety of competitive processes and channels for the expression of interests and values—associational as well as partisan, functional as well as territorial, collective as well as individual. All are integral to its practice.[4]

Insofar as such conceptions prevail, in any society or relatively stable constitutional democratic regime, the tensions among the different conceptions of democracy may indeed be attenuated. But even in such regimes these tensions are always simmering, ready, as it were, to erupt in situations of intensive change. This possibility is inherent in modern constitutional democratic regimes because the different conceptions of democracy analyzed and the tensions among them are embedded in their basic premises and in their historical and ideological roots. Moreover, the different conceptions of democracy are closely interwoven with the political process that developed within these regimes and are articulated in this process. Structural characteristics of this political process include first the emergence of a new type of political class or classes, the means whereby political support is mobilized, and the relations between this mobilization and governance as manifest in the promulgation of policies and their implementation. Second, there is the potential politicization of many social conflicts, to continual redefinitions of the appropriate scope of political action and of the boundaries of the political, and third, the centrality of social movement and protest movements in this process. Let me elaborate here on these points.[5]

The development of modern regimes was connected, first, with the emergence of a new type of nonascriptive, semiprofessional political class or classes, the members of which compete openly for power and for broader political support. Second, it was connected with the development of organizations for mobilizing support among the electorate, the most important of which in modern societies have been political parties and interest groups working through representatives (such as lobby groups), as well as social and political movements. This development was also connected with the close relations between the promulgation of policies, the regulation of conflicts, and the process of selecting rulers and with the fact that these processes have been played out, with the partial exception of some of the city-states of antiquity, the public domain, in "the open" and under continuous public scrutiny.

But it is only these characteristics in combination with two additional ones that can explain the full impact of the confrontations among the different conceptions of democracy on the dynamics of these regimes. These are, first, the generally high level, unparalleled in other regimes (with the possible partial exception of some of the city-states of antiquity), of potential politicization of many problems and demands of various sectors of the society and of conflicts among them and, second, the continual struggle about the redefinition of the realm of the political.

The tendency to the politicization of social conflicts has been manifest first in the continual interweaving of struggles about various concrete issues, of discrete interests of individuals and groups, with struggles surrounding the promulgation of different conceptions of common will, of visions of the good society. Contrary to the assumptions of many rational choice analyses, the mobilization of political support has not in modern societies been based only on the aggregation of discrete interests. Very often this mobilization focuses, as Alessandro Pizzorno has shown and has been fully illustrated by numerous new social movements, on symbols of political, social, ethnic, or gender identity as well as on closely related conceptions of the common good, usually couched and legitimated in primordial and sacral terms.[6]

It is in close relation to such interweaving of concrete demands and interests on the one hand and, on the other hand, of conceptions of common identity and of the common good that there developed in all modern regimes the strong tendency to continually redefine the boundaries of what is considered as the appropriate scope of political action, the boundaries of the realm of the political, of the legitimate, open political arena. The drawing of the boundaries of the political has in itself constituted one of the major foci of open political contestation and struggle, promoted above all by various social movements—albeit, of course, often in conjunction with other political actors. The transition from the laissez-faire conception of the state—never, of course, fully realized—to post–Second World War Keynesian regulatory policies and the institutionalization of the welfare state is perhaps the best illustration of such redefinition, but it constitutes only the tip of the iceberg.[7] In fact such changes have been continuous in modern societies throughout their histories.

Such redefinitions of the political usually do entail, as the example of the welfare state attests, the reconstruction of the conception of common good and of the rights and entitlements of the members of the community to public distribution of private goods, especially access to public goods, and consequently changes in the relative strength of different centers of power in the society, of the relations between civil society and the state, and between what is defined as private realms as against public arenas.

The demands for the reconstruction of the realm of the political usually involved the articulation of the basic tensions inherent in the modern constitutional democratic regimes and the concomitant tension among the different conceptions of democracy, especially between the constitutional and the participatory conceptions. At the same time, demands for the reconstruction of the realm of the political highlighted the tensions between equality and liberty, between ideas of individual rights and the primacy of majoritarian decision, between the routine and the revolutionary aspects of politics,[8] between the Jacobin and pluralistic components in political program of modernity, between the autonomy of civil society and the state, and between the self-legitimacy of the rules of the constitutional game and legitimation in some other, often "ultimate" vision couched in primordial or sacral-religious terms.

3

The most central, although certainly not the only type of modern political organization that promulgated demands for changes in the boundaries of the political and articulated tensions and themes of protest inherent in the cultural and political program of modernity were the various social movements that developed in the modern regimes. These movements constituted the transformation, in the modern setting, of the various heterodoxies of the Axial civilizations, especially those that sought to realize, by political action, the Kingdom of God on earth. These different movements constituted in modern societies one of the main, perhaps *the* main, bearers of utopian visions and of the search for their implementation, a search that constituted a central, if certainly not the only component of the modern political discourse and process. Many of these movements laid a very strong emphasis on social and cultural activism, on the ability of man to reconstruct society.

This emphasis was closely connected to the charismatization of the center as the major arena in which such visions can and should be implemented and to the concomitant continual interaction between center and periphery and the tendency to the incorporation of symbols of protest in the center that developed in these societies. One central repercussion of this orientation to the center was the development of ideological politics, most fully epitomized in the ideological distinction between left and right.

4

Several types of social movements developed in modern Europe and then in the Americas, then later in Asian and African societies. One major type was center oriented, with the major aim of reconstructing the centers and the boundaries of their respective societies and the implementation of which was perceived as embodying the most important charismatic dimensions of the modern socio-cultural order.[9]

Among such center-oriented movements were, first, those that aimed at changing the distribution of power and its bases within a given society. The most important of these were those that aimed at the growing inclusion, through the extension of suffrage, of wider strata into the central political framework, and the socialist and communist movements that combined such demands with demands for reconstruction of the center, especially for weakening the hierarchical premises thereof and of the patterns of political economy. The second major type of such movements were those that aimed at reconstructing the boundaries of the respective political collectivities, above all the national or nationalistic and ethnic ones.

But such center-oriented movements were not the only ones that developed in modern societies. Alongside them were religious reform and cooperative or syndicalist movements that aimed at the reorganization of some aspects of life among different sectors of society, many popular movements that emphasized autonomous participation in the political process as against bureaucratic or center domination, as well as anarchist movements that opposed the state in principle. Many of the movements not oriented to the center emphasize the construction of new spaces to some extent independent of the center, but sometimes also impinging on it. In most movements there always existed some overlap between orientation to the center and construction of new spaces. The concrete themes they promulgated could in later periods or in other situations become transposed into center-oriented ones. Thus for instance many contemporary social movements—the women's movement and the movements of various minorities, all demanding changes in allocation of resources and access to them—have become more and more oriented to the center.[10] Similarly, many fundamentalist and religious communal movements have, in the last decades of the twentieth century, become among the most important center-oriented movements. All these movements usually promulgate not only specific demands but combine them with broader, overarching visions that often entail strong Jacobin components.

Within all these movements the major tensions inherent in the modern political process were continually articulated, especially the tensions between the collective Jacobin or communal and the pluralistic components thereof, between different conceptions of the relations between the general will and the will of all, between the primordial or sacred and the civil components of their legitimation, between control and freedom or autonomy.

5

The nature of these movements and their impact on the political dynamics of their respective societies can be understood only against the background of specific, but continually changing, historical conditions and processes within which the modern cultural and political program, with its tensions and contradictions, continually developed. As we have seen, the most important among these processes have been the formation of new types of collectivities; the development of new state-society relations most fully manifest in the emergence of a multiplicity of centers of power and of distinct types of civil society; the transformation of center-periphery relations and of political processes; the development of capitalist, later industrial-capitalist, types of political economy; the concomitant emergence of the European state system; and the development, with European expansion, of worldwide institutional and symbolic frameworks and systems. All these institutional developments constituted not only the historical background against which the cultural and political programs of modernity developed, but—as indicated above—also the arenas in which these programs, with the antinomies, tensions, and contradictions inherent in them, were continually played out. It was the ongoing tensions and contradictions between the basic premises of the cultural and political programs of modernity, and between these premises and the developments within the various national and international institutional arenas, that gave rise to the major social movements.

6

The concrete contours of these major social movements—their ideologies, their major actors, the bases of their support, and the extent of their being center oriented—have been continually changing in different modern societies, but most, possibly all, these movements addressed themselves critically to different components or dimensions of the political and cultural programs of modernity and to the basic tensions and antinomies inherent in them and their institutionalization in different historical settings and contexts. All these movements entailed specific modes of selection from among the major themes of the cultural program of modernity, their political and institutional repercussions and their continual interpretations. Thus, for instance, criticisms of the existing order of modernity put forward by the socialist movements were mostly couched in terms of the noncompletion of this program and oriented toward its fuller implementation. The national movements built on those components of the revolutionary heritage that emphasized the right to self-determination of a collectivity. They aimed above all at the reconstruction of the boundaries of newly emerging collectivities, advocating highly particularistic primordial terms. They entailed the confrontation between the universalistic and more particularistic or ascriptive components of legitimation of the modern regimes. Their criticism of the existing order could develop in the direction of a more extreme negation of the universalistic components of the cultural program of modernity and then of the concomitant institutional premises of pluralistic regimes. Extreme nationalist movements denied the universal and universalistic orientations of these regimes and espoused primordial racial orientations in an extremely ideological way. Unlike the conservative movements predominant throughout most of the nineteenth century on the right wing of the political spectrum, these new extreme nationalist movements evinced strong Jacobin mobilisatory tendencies, i.e. to mobilize people for concerted, above all political action. Later, contemporary fundamentalist movements put forward extreme anti-Enlightenment ideologies together with very strong Jacobin participatory and mobilisatory orientations.

These continually changing movements developed side by side, often complementing but also often competing with one another. They were complementary as they were rooted in the common historical experience of their societies and of modern international systems. But different movements developed in conjunction with different dimensions of this experience and emphasized different problems and contradictions between the premises of this program and its institutionalization. They promoted different visions of modern life, of the modern social and political order, and of modernity. Accordingly, they could also under some conditions oppose and contradict one another and come into intensive ideological and political conflict with one another, as was the case in the fierce struggle between communist and fascist movements in the 1930s or between communist and liberal democratic ideologies during the Cold War. These various movements posed the most important challenges to the newly emerging constitutional regimes. They first challenged those regimes that developed in reaction against the ancient regimes and later challenged, possibly to a greater extent, various postrevolutionary regimes. It was in the continual encounter between these movements and the different regimes in which they developed that the basic characteristics—as well as problems, tensions, and contradictions—of the political program of modernity became fully articulated.

CHAPTER SEVEN

SOCIAL MOVEMENTS IN MODERN CONSTITUTIONAL REGIMES

I

Social movements and the challenges they posed to modern constitutional and constitutional democratic regimes developed in all these regimes, yet the contours of these movements, their themes, and the demands they promulgated, as well as their impact, have varied greatly. While a full-fledged comparative analysis of such variations would be, of course, beyond the scope of this essay, some indications may not be out of place.

Let me illustrate the major differences in, to follow Charles Tilly's terminology,[1] the repertoire of themes put forward by various movements and their impact on their respective societies as they developed in two "old" societies and states, Europe and Japan, and two relatively "new" societies or states, the United States and Israel, with brief allusion to India, the only continual constitutional democracy among the new postcolonial states that built on both the precolonial tradition and colonial (British) traditions.

One of the most important differences from the point of view of our discussion has been between, on the one hand, those societies, such as Japan or certain states in Europe, in which the very access to the modern centers—that is, of citizenship and representation—constituted a major focus of struggle and, on the other hand, those like the United States, Israel, or India in which access to the centers was given to all members of the community, however such membership was defined. Both in Europe and in Japan movements aiming at extending suffrage (that is, fighting for participation and access to the political center), constituted a continual component of the political arena. Such movements developed among different social groups, first among the rising middle class, then among the working class; some movements also represented religious groups (for instance Catholics in England) and, of course, women. In contrast, in the United States, Israel, and India, such movements did not, except in the early period of the United States, develop. In India and Israel citizenship was granted immediately with the establishment of the state. In the United States, suffrage was extended shortly after the founding, with the crucial exception of the African Americans and, as was in this period the case throughout the world, of women.

2

Some of these differences among Europe, Japan, the United States, Israel, and India are due to differences in their historical background, in the development of constitutional and democratic institutions and regimes within them, and in the historical timing of their transitions to democracy. Of special importance in this context is the fact that both in Europe and in Japan constitutional, later democratic regimes developed out of absolutist regimes with strong feudal roots, while that was not the case in the United States, Israel, or India. In Europe and Japan access to political power was closely related to the differential status of different groups with their respective feudal heritages. In India, movements for independence and union had done away with most of the earlier colonial and some pseudofeudal elements. In the United States and Israel such elements were from the beginning very weak or nonexistent.

But historical timing alone does not explain the differences between Europe and Japan on the one hand, and the United States, Israel, and India on the other, as well as the differences among the last three societies. In these three, the granting of universal or almost universal suffrage was inherent in some of the basic premises—especially those of political equality—of their respective regimes even if the social and cultural meaning of equality differed greatly among them. Accordingly, in contrast to European countries and to Japan, the construction of the center did not entail the ideological confrontation between equality and hierarchy.

One of the most important results in those societies of the granting of universal suffrage was that, in contrast to European countries and Japan, social, economic, and to some extent also ethnic or national problems were not usually combined with those of access to the political center. It was only with respect to some groups not seen as being full members of the broader collectivity—native Americans and African Americans in the United States, Arabs in Israel, and some tribal groups in India—that some connections between ethnic or national questions and access to citizenship developed. But on the whole the problems of access to citizenship, of political equality, and of participation did not become in these three countries closely interwoven with social and economic problems attendant on the development of industrialization and of capitalist or semicapitalist political economies.

Accordingly, yet another most interesting outcome of these differences between Europe and Japan, on the one hand, and the United States, Israel, and India, on the other, has been the place of socialist movements. Socialist movements were not important movements of protest in the United States, Israel, or India. In these countries the basic acceptance of political equality and the lack of confrontation between equality and hierarchy in the construction of the center undermined one of the basic raisons d'etre of socialist movements as they developed in Europe.

In Israel this fact was paradoxically connected with a basic aspect of its historical experience: pioneering groups with strong labor-socialist orientations were among the founders of Israeli society and constituted for a very long period its ruling elite.[2] In India socialism was to some extent espoused by the Congress ruling elite but not by the most important social and political movements. The various particularistic, caste, linguistic, and territorial groups raised claims for redistribution of resources for their members, but not in universalistic terms oriented to the (semi-utopian) reconstruction of the center.[3] In the United States the very definition of the overall community in utopian, universalistic, future-oriented terms knocked the props out from under socialism.[4]

3

At the same time the ways in which the problems of access to citizenship were defined and combined with economic, social, ethnic, or national problems differed greatly among various European countries and between Europe and Japan. In Europe the protest movements that were the bearers of such demands—above all the socialist and nationalist movements—were oriented very strongly to the reconstruction of the center in terms of the confrontation between equality and hierarchy. Moreover, the symbols and components of collective identity of their respective societies and their relative importance varied greatly among European countries. In Japan, attempts at the reconstruction of the center and of the components of collective identity were very weak, promulgated mostly by marginal groups that were not able to mobilize widespread support. The major orientation—and impact of protest movements in Japan, which on the face of it were very similar to European movements—was the creation of new social and cultural spaces in which different groups could develop relatively autonomous activities and collective identities. It is not that the various movements in Europe did not construct such spaces; indeed probably in purely quantitative terms this was their major impact. But at least until lately the major challenge to the constitutional democratic regimes in Europe came from movements oriented to the reconstruction of their respective centers and collective identities. Another important difference between Europe and Japan was that in Japan there were barely any national or ethnic movements. Only lately have there been some developments in this direction among the Ainu and the Burakumin. But even these movements seem to be oriented mainly to the creation of legitimate spaces for these ethnic groups, in which their distinctiveness and identity ought to be recognized without necessarily being oriented to the reconstruction of the center.[5]

Similarly, the protest movements that did develop in those societies in which socialist movements did not develop or were very weak—the United States, Israel, and India—varied greatly. In the United States these movements were above all moralistic, populist, and reformist, and their ethnic components were often, even if only implicitly, very important. In Israel the predominant movements emphasized reconstruction of the symbols of collective identity, often in combination with demands for active participation of broader groups (such as various groups of new immigrants) in the center and with different stances with respect to the Palestinian Arabs and Arab states.[6] In India movements based on caste and regional and linguistic identity were the most important.

4

In addition to aspects of their historical experiences mentioned above, these differences between Europe and Japan, as well as those among the

United States, Israel, and India, were rooted in some of the basic premises and institutional implications of their respective civilizations, thus highlighting the importance of the civilizational dimension of these societies for understanding the development and dynamics of modern constitutional democratic regimes.

Let me illustrate the importance of these dimensions by a very brief excursus about Japan and the United States. The focus of this excursus will be the impact of the basic patterns of collective identity on the political process and on protest movements, an aspect of the constitution of modern societies that is, as we shall see later, of crucial importance for understanding the fate of constitutional democratic regimes.

From the point of view of our analysis the more important aspect of the construction of Japanese collective identity was its emphasis on the embeddedness of the major arenas of social action in contexts defined in some combinations of natural, sacral, or primordial terms. This collective identity defined Japan as a sacral liturgical community and emphasized the sacredness and uniqueness of the Japanese collectivity or nation. This concept of a divine nation—or to follow R.J.Z. Werblowsky's felicitous expression, of sacred particularity[7]—did not entail, as was the case in monotheistic religions and civilizations, the connotation of being uniquely "chosen" in terms of a transcendental and universalistic mission; neither did it entail the idea of responsibility to God to behave according to certain precepts or commandments.

This conception of sacred particularity usually held its own when confronted with the universalistic ideologies of Axial civilizations or religions that impinged on Japan—Buddhism, Confucianism, or, in recent times, modern ideologies such as liberalism, constitutionalism, progressivism or Marxism—all of which seemingly called for a redefinition of the symbols of collective identity in some universal direction. With the exception of small groups of intellectuals, this redefinition did not put down roots in the Japanese collective consciousness. Instead, the premises of these religions or ideologies were reconstructed in Japan in a combination of sacral, primordial, and natural terms. At the same time, the terms themselves were continuously reformulated in a way that would allow for the incorporation of new themes. This construction of Japanese collective identity has been closely related to the specific definitions of the major arenas of social life that have been prevalent in Japan. The primary characteristics of this definition have been the strong emphasis on contextual frameworks and the concomitant relative weakness of fully formalized, abstract rules demarcating clearly between the different arenas of action and defining them in abstract, formal terms as separate entities. Social actors—whether individuals or institutional arenas—have been defined in their relation to other such actors not as autonomous ontological entities but in terms of their mutual interweaving in common frameworks or contexts. Any institutional arena—political, economic, family, or different arenas of cultural production, such as art, literature, or any group or organization—has been defined in terms of its relation to the social nexus in which it was embedded. Such nexus was defined in some—continuously changing—combination of primordial, sacral, natural, and ascriptive terms that were not defined in relation to any principles transcending them.

Concomitantly, the major arenas of social action have not been regulated, above all, by distinct autonomous, legal, bureaucratic, or voluntary organization or rules—even if such organizations have developed within them—but mostly through various less formal arrangements and networks that have in their turn usually been embedded in various ascriptively defined, and continuously redefined, social contexts, of which the national collectivity was the most encompassing.

One crucial derivative of this definition of the Japanese collectivity was the impossibility of becoming Japanese by conversion. The Buddhist sects or Confucian schools—the most natural candidates for channels of conversation—could not serve as such in Japan.[8]

These conceptions of the Japanese collectivity entailed very intensive orientations to the "other"—to China, Asia, and the West—and an awareness of other encompassing civilizations claiming some universal validity.[9] But they did not entail the participation of the Japanese collectivity in such civilizations and its reconstruction according to universalistic premises. They did not generate, at least not within Japan, the perception of Japan becoming one, even if possibly a central, component of such a universalistic framework. At most they entailed the assertion that the Japanese collectivity embodied the pristine values enunciated by other civilizations, which were wrongfully appropriated by them. At the same time this conception involved a very strong tendency, which played an important role in the Japanese society from the Meiji up to the contemporary period, to define the Japanese collectivity in terms of "incomparable" uniqueness, very often couched in semiracial, genetic terms, or in terms of some special, distinct, Japanese spirituality.

This specific mode of construction of collective identity has had several repercussions on the structuring of the political arena and on some of the distinctive characteristics of Japan as a modern polity. The most important of these have been the development, first of a weak concept of the state as distinct from the broader overall, in modern terms national community ("national" being defined in sacral, natural, and primordial terms), and second of a societal state characterized by a strong tendency to emphasize guidance rather than direct regulation and the permeation of the periphery by the center. These conceptions of state and civil society entailed the conflation of both state and civil society and their embedment in the national community.

Such conflation of the national community and the state, and the concomitant weakness of distinct conceptions of the state of civil society, had already developed in the Sengoku and Tokugawa periods and in the concept of *kokutai* and can be seen in the modern and contemporary periods in the slogan "united monarch and people" (*kunmin dochii*) and in the closely related distinction between *kokutai* (national structure) and *seitai* (political structure) that makes the latter inferior to the former and embedded in it.[10]

Concomitantly there developed in Japan a strong tendency to the conflation of different occupational or class sectors within the different social contexts, be they enterprises, neighborhoods, or such frameworks as various new religions, above all within the context of the national community. The same was to a very large extent true of the basic conception of economic activities, which were legitimated not in transcendental terms but in terms of their contribution to their respective settings or to the overall collectivity. At the same time, the major elites were embedded in broader settings or contexts, defined in some combination of primordial, sacral, and natural terms in which symbols of kinship were often predominant. Within such contexts, and in conjunction with the far-reaching structural differentiation, mobility, and openness, there developed a very intensive dynamic, the best known outcome of which were the educational and economic miracles of modern Japan. But it was in many ways a dynamics highly regulated in primordial, social, and natural terms.

Closely related has been a very weak development of an autonomous civil society, although needless to say elements of the latter, especially the structural components thereof (such as different organizations) have not been missing. One of the most interesting corollaries of this embedment of the political arena and of civil society alike within the overall community has been the absence in the historical (feudal) and early modern conceptions of autonomous legal rights and of representative institutions. In Japan, however, unlike in many absolutist or totalitarian systems, the absence of such institutions was not connected with a strong symbolic distinction of the center, of the state, or with strong efforts by the center not only to control but also to restructure and mobilize the periphery—according to a new vision destructive of the values hitherto prevalent in the periphery. Thus no social, economic, or political sectors could easily develop a principled autonomy or autonomous claims to access to the center, although it was very difficult for autonomous public spaces not confronting the center cult to develop. It was these characteristics of the political arena in Japan that explain some of the distinctive characteristics of Japan's social movements, including the new religions, especially their relatively nonideological challenges and nonconfrontational stances to the center.

5

I shall complement this brief excursus on Japan with one on American civilization. This excursus will, first, illustrate that the basic civilizational premises and the mode of construction of collective identity that developed in the United States differed from the European experience, thus attesting to the fact that within the West there developed different programs of modernity, and, second, compare it—even if briefly—with the Japanese case. The collective identity or consciousness that developed in American civilization was based on a political ideology transformed from a religious experience but maintaining its religious orientations, a hitherto unique occurrence in the history of mankind. Unlike the case in the Roman Empire, where the common citizenship was defined in secular-legal terms, with some undertones of a common cultural ambiance, in the United States the religious roots and components of the common bond were crucial.

The American civilization and "way of life" were constructed in terms of a common political ideology with religious components and an emphasis on Christian heritage and with almost no territorial or historical components, rather than, as was the case in Europe, in terms of a combination of religious tradition with historical, ethnic, or national identity. This collective consciousness was not related to a common historical origin, to common historical memory, mythical or actual—that is, it did not comprise strong primordial components. Instead, it was the rather specific type of civil religion, as defined by Robert N. Bellah,[11] that constituted the core of this collective identity. Concomitantly, the premises of this civilization entailed the constitution of a social order, of a collectivity the identity of which was not couched in hierarchical terms and in which the problems of the hierarchical aspects of the society were not related to the problems of the constitution of the body politic.

Religion played a central and rather paradoxical role in the construction and dynamics of American cultural and political programs, collective consciousness, and identity. The paradoxical nature of this role has been manifest in the fact that on the one hand these programs have to no small extent developed from religious, above all Protestant, traditions, from the strong totalistic components thereof, while on the other hand one of their major institutional derivations has been the separation of Church and State. This separation was not based on secular, antireligious premises, which could be found in the Enlightenment. Rather, insofar as it was rooted in the Enlightenment, it was based on the deistic premises and above all on the strong opposition to any established (State) Church as part of the opposition to strong government. Second, the separation was rooted in the historical experience of escaping from the wars of religion and the resulting recognition that it was impossible to impose any single religion on a multiplicity of sects. This recognition gave rise to strong emphasis on religious tolerance among different religious groups, even if in some of the first colonies the established church was initially institutionalized. Thus religion was seemingly pushed into the realm of the private, but in fact it was pushed into the nongovernmental associational public area, where it played a most central role and thus also in the political arena. As Wendy F. Naylor has put it, the separation of Church and State did not necessarily entail the separation of religion from politics.[12] Religious symbols and discourse constituted a continual component of the public and political discourse. A central element here was the need to preserve the purity of the American commonwealth against the various attempts of the forces of evil threatening it from the inside or outside—a theme repeated again and again by American politicians, from Abraham Lincoln and Theodore Roosevelt to Jimmy Carter and Ronald Reagan. Similarly, American individualism was very often cast in religious terms and symbols. Above all the religious component was continually interwoven with the reinterpretation of American collective consciousness or identity, and at the same time the construction of this identity constituted a central part of the agenda of many religious associations and activities in the United States.

This rather unusual place of the religious components in the construction of American collective identity has been very closely related to the special attitudes to authority and to the basic institutional frameworks, especially to the Constitution, that developed in the United States. The strong religious, utopian dimension of the American cultural and political programs and their ideological format gave rise to one of the most important aspects of American society. This is the combination of, on the one hand, a very strong and emphatic acceptance of the basic institutional, especially constitutional, framework with, on the other hand, a very strong suspicion of those in authority and a distrust of the government. This combination generated a special combination of moralism and pragmatism in political life. The overall community—the republic or commonwealth—and its basic institutional-symbolic frameworks tended to become the foci of the charismatic, utopian dimension or orientation, of the search for the pure community, of the covenant binding it together, while the concrete political institutions, processes, and officeholders could easily become the foci of mistrust. Fear of government expansion has constituted a continuing theme in American political discourse. Such mistrust was closely connected to the very strong populist orientations prevalent in the United States and could give rise to the search for participatory politics seemingly undiluted by the political process—a theme promulgated recently by Ross Perot, as his emphasis on symbolic electronic town meetings attests.

Concomitantly there developed in the United States a rather unusual combination of the center being defined much more in terms of the overall community, of the republic with its constitutional arrangements, and much less in terms of the concrete political institutions. This combination could sometimes be seen in different designations of the country. "America" would often be used to designate the overall community, the bearer of the strong utopian vision, while "the United States" would designate the more mundane concrete governmental institution.[13]

This attitude to authority was very closely related to a more general characteristic of American politics and political discourse—a continual oscillation between, on the one hand, a pragmatic, realistic attitude most fully epitomized in pork-barrel politics and in a very unsentimental, sometimes brutal attitude to the political game, and on the other hand in a highly moralistic, often missionary, self-justifying, and sanctimonious attitude. This oscillation generated in the United States, in Samuel P. Huntington's words, a promise of disharmony,[14] but a disharmony based on full acceptance of the premises of the center and of the search for the reestablishment of the utopian harmony inherent in these premises.

6

All these factors are very important in explaining the major characteristic of the protest movements that developed in the United States. Protest was indeed built into the very premises and institutional framework of the American political system as promulgated in its "myth" or creed. It was the basic American political and constitutional discourse, and its tensions that have also provided the basic framework of themes and protest movements that developed very early and continue today.

Most of these movements shared the basic premises of the American cultural program: its strong future orientation, messianism, this-worldliness, emphasis on active participation, and commitment to the social order. These themes of protest were strongly interwoven with constitutional and legal debates and discourses, thus greatly reinforcing the acceptance by most of these movements of the basic premises of American civilization.

Whatever the differences among these movements, they were not oriented to the reconstruction of the center and of the community but rather to their purification, to bringing them up to the fuller realization of the utopian vision of the American community. Indeed, the most distinctive characteristic of the major protest movements that developed in the United States was that they were above all oriented to upholding the premises of the American vision, which constituted a central component of the American collective consciousness and political creed.

The major themes of protest that developed in the United States were set very firmly within the basic parameters of the American political and constitutional discourse. These themes, found in revivalist movements, in the abolitionist movement, and in the movements of displaced farmers and of industrial workers that developed in nineteenth century, focused on identifying the evils threatening the basic premises of the American system. They were oriented against those aspects of society that were seen as contaminating the purity of American life and sought to eliminate the pollution. The two most important evils exposed by many such movements, and in the general political discourse, were, first, unbridled egoism and, second, the concentration of power and wealth. Both were seen as undermining the basic foundation of American life, of the covenant that brings the American people together. The negation of the inequality generated by concentration of wealth or power was couched not in class terms but in such terms as producers as against "parasites" or, later in the twentieth century, in terms of denial to large sectors of society of access to the fruits of good life and to full and equal participation in the political and moral life of the community. This attitude did not entail the principled negation of inequality, only of those extreme manifestations of inequality that were perceived as an outcome of evil forces.

These themes, which were very often couched in terms of the basic premises of the American creed and constitutional discourse, were upheld by almost all the protest movements that developed in the United States. Each movement naturally emphasized different themes and combined them with different concrete social and economic problems and demands, which naturally varied greatly in different periods. Rightist movements tended to advocate the view that the way to fight the pollution of the American vision was to uphold traditional values, while leftist movements tended to advocate opening up to new experience and visions.

7

The comparison between Europe and Japan and between Europe and the United States—without even going into parallel comparisons with India and Israel—indicates how differences in the historical experience of these societies and in their civilizational premises, in the conception of cosmic and social orders held by different elites in continual interaction with the major sectors of the society, have influenced the development of major institutional formations of these societies, the structure and orientations of different protest movements and their impact on the political arena, the timing and definition or formulation of the major issues that were raised by these movements, and the ways in which they touched on the central nerves of different political regimes and constituted major challenges for them.

Thus, to give only a few illustrations of some ideal types of such movements: Movements focused on the reconstruction of centers, which were most predominant in Europe, tend to develop above all in societies with strong tensions among the different components of collective identity, especially among primordial, civil, and universalistic tensions defined in transcendental terms, as well as between the premises of hierarchy and equality in the constitution of the center. Such movements tend to develop when these tensions are exacerbated and there is a lag between the timing of the constitution of political units (states) and of different national collectivities. Movements oriented to more fully implementing the basic premises of the center, without challenging these premises, develop, as was the case above all in the United States, when access to the centers of economic power are seen as blocked by groups or forces that have been perceived subverting these premises. Movements oriented to the creation of new social spaces tend to develop especially in those societies and situations in which the premises of the societal order and of collective identities are taken for granted and are not challenged by ideological visions and in which the center is perceived mostly in pragmatic terms—either as to some extent the United States, where the visions promulgated by the center are accepted by most sectors of the society, or as in India, where the ideological component is not central in the premises of the center.

Various European countries, the United States, and Japan constitute illustrations of these three ideal types. Israel is, from this point of view, a mixed case in which the acceptance of many of the premises of the centers was combined with strong attempts at the reconstruction of components of collective identity. In fact, within each of these societies there developed great variations, and different nontypical types of movements could become predominant under appropriate conditions in some periods, situations, or sectors of the society.

Such movements are organized by coalitions of different elites, such as political elites, the bearers of ideological visions, and the promoters of the solidarity of different sectors and representatives of economic interests. The relative importance of these different elites and the nature of the relations among them vary, however, in different movements and in different situations. It was especially the relations among political elites, the promoters of solidarity of different collectivities, and autonomous intellectuals that have been the most distinctive characteristic of different movements. Such relative importance is influenced among other factors by the premises and historical experiences of the respective societies and by the concrete political regimes in which they develop. Thus, to give some very brief illustration, the importance of autonomous intellectuals in their relation to political elites and to the promoters of the solidarity of different sectors of society is smaller in societies in which there is a strong emphasis on civility and in which the national collectivities and modern political centers developed more or less in tandem and before the onset of democratization. It is also relatively small in societies, like Japan, in which the sacral components of the collective identity are not defined in transcendental terms, or in societies like India, in which sacral components are not focused on the political arena, or in societies like the United States (and also India and Japan), in which the basic premises of the political order have not been challenged, or in societies, again like the United States (and Japan), in which the basic premises of the center are not challenged. In contrast, the role of autonomous intellectual elites is greater in societies in which there is a strong tension between the primordial and sacral components of the collective identity and between hierarchical and egalitarian orientations.

Carriers of the solidarity of different collectivities who advocate different conceptions of collective identity become of special importance when there develops an important temporal gap between the construction of national collectivities and new states.

The preceding are only a few illustrative—and tentative—indications about the orientations and compositions of different social movements, and also indications for further research.

THE CHALLENGE OF INCORPORATING PROTEST: THE NON-ZERO-SUM GAME CONCEPTION OF POLITICS AND THE STRUCTURING OF TRUST IN MODERN SOCIETIES

I

Whatever their differences, social movements developed within all modern societies, and most visibly constitutional and constitutional democratic regimes, posed, as we have seen, the most important challenges to the newly emerging regimes. The ubiquity of these movements and the concomitant challenges of the contradiction between an encompassing, totalistic, potentially totalitarian vision and a commitment to pluralistic premises constituted an inherent element of all modern regimes and a basic component of their political dynamics. None of the modern constitutional and/or liberal democracies has entirely done away—or can do away—with either the Jacobin component, especially in its utopian dimension, or with orientations to some primordial or religious components of collective identity and of the legitimatization of the political order.

With these challenges, the modern constitutional democratic regimes face a double ideological and institutional jeopardy. There is, first, the possibility that the promulgators of the general will may deny the legitimacy of the pluralism inherent in the articulation of the "will of all." Second, there is the possibility that different conceptions of the general will may develop and struggle against one another for hegemony.

These jeopardies focus the most important problems these regimes face on the very bases of constitutional democracy, beyond adherence to the rules of the game. The first problem is to create and maintain some common framework in which different views of the common good can compete without undermining the very possibility of the working of the system. The second problem is not just the assurance that the major political actors will adhere to the existing rules of the game but the capacity to incorporate protest, to redefine the boundaries of the political, and to transform the bases of legitimation in these regimes.

Incorporating protest entails reconstructing of *volonté générale*—the common will or the good social order. In this way these regimes may become transformed and their continuity maintained, without giving up the constitutional frameworks and the basic premises of democracy. Incorporating the demands, themes, and symbols promulgated by protest movements, the reconstruction of the *volonté générale* may develop in several often overlapping directions; first, the reconstruction of the symbols of collective identity and of centers; second, the redefinition of at least some of the premises and the patterns of legitimation; third, implementation of policies aiming at the redistribution of resources and public entitlements; and fourth, the construction of social spaces in which different groups can develop distinctive patterns of social, cultural, or economic activities and advance their specific identities.

2

The fact that many constitutional democratic regimes have foundered exactly because they were unable to incorporate symbols and themes of protest and different sectors of the population into their central institutional frameworks underscores their inherent fragility. The roots of this fragility lie in the fact that, as Adam Przeworski has pointed out,[1] the nature of the political struggle in these regimes entails uncertainty about the outcome of any single political contest, of any single election, or of any single dispute about the implementation of policies. In other words, no political actor can be sure of the outcome of the political contest. In the best case he or she can only be sure of being given a second chance at the next stage of the political process or "game."

Such uncertainty is rooted first of all in the basic openness of the political process and the multiplicity of goals that are fundamental to these regimes. True enough, at any given period the range of political goals is not limitless; some major issues are in the forefront of political struggle, while others are suppressed or bracketed out. The range of goal is also limited by the relation between capitalism and constitutional democracy. One of the criticisms of constitutional democratic regimes, voiced especially from the left, is that they were never able to transcend the capitalist order, while others, at least until lately mostly on the right, claimed that a market economy was a *sine qua non* for constitutional democracies. Without entering into this debate, suffice it to point out that the capitalist regimes of the late twentieth century are far removed from those of the nineteenth or the early twentieth century, that at the very least they have been tamed or transformed in far-reaching ways very much under the impact of socialist movements. Socialism has changed the range of political goals in society,[2] thus exemplifying the process of incorporating protest, and of extending the range of political goals. Thus it is the nature of constitutional democratic regimes, and above all in the historical conditions of their formation and subsequent development, that the ranges of political goals have been continuously—even if not endlessly—changing. These very facts introduce a strong element of uncertainty into the political game, which is indeed at the root of the fragility of these regimes.

This uncertainty and fragility are closely related to two central characteristics of the modern political process that are to be found in all modern but especially in constitutional democratic regimes and are closely related to the protest movements referred to above. These problems are related, first, to the generally high potential, unparalleled in any other regimes (with the partial exception of some of the city-states of antiquity), for the politicization of the problems and demands of various sectors of society and for conflicts among them. Second, they are related to the continual attempts at redefining the realm of the political. In all these regimes the boundaries of what is to be considered as the appropriate scope of political action, the boundaries of the political, of the legitimate, open political arena, have been continually changing and constitute one of the major foci of open political contestation and struggle.

3

Problems arise from the openness of the political process in modern constitutional democratic regimes and the uncertainty of political outcomes;

the calls for the incorporation of demands and themes of protest, which necessarily involve claims for rather far-reaching redistribution of resources in society and far-reaching changes in the relative strength of different groups or sectors of the society, exacerbate the possibility that those in positions of relative power will not be willing to give up their positions. The possibility that they will give up such positions, that they will accept the chance that they may lose at least some of their power through the process of incorporating protest, can develop only insofar as they come to believe that such loss is only temporary and that these positions, or equivalent ones, may be regained later through the same political process.

Here we come to a central paradox in the constitution and dynamics of constitutional democratic regimes—namely, that the possibility of the power holders' accepting the demands of various social movements is paradoxically infused in the very openness of the political process in these societies, in the very existence of multiplicity of political actors, and in the tendency for the boundaries of the political realm to change continuously. While such openness and the concomitant multiplicity and changeability of political goals give rise to the very causes that create potential instability of these regimes, they may also, paradoxically, under appropriate conditions, generate the possibility of transformation and therefore the continuity of these regimes.

The crux of this paradox lies in the fact that the very openness of the political process characteristic of these regimes gives rise to the development in them of non-zero-sum conceptions of the political struggle. In most political regimes the political game has been perceived as a zero-sum game. The gain of any one contender or group of contenders at any given moment means the loss by others. The margins of survival in this game are narrow. In contrast, in the modern constitutional democratic regimes, the range of potential political game and struggle has been continuously expanding—possibly up to the point at which the very nature of the game may have changed. It may, indeed, no longer be a zero-sum game and no longer be perceived as such.

The development of this non-zero-sum conception of politics, with its strong future orientation, may permit major political actors to give up some of the positions of power they hold according to the constitutional rules of the game. Thus the prevalence of the non-zero-sum conception may generate within modern constitutional democratic regimes the capacity to incorporate new demands and symbols of protest, thus increasing their potential for transformation.

This possibility epitomizes the paradox of modern constitutional democratic regimes. The crux of the paradox lies in the fact that any transformation entails the acceptance by most political actors of some "metalegitimation" beyond the existing rules of the game, but at the same time the transformation has to be effected within the framework of the very institutions through which the rules of the game are laid down.

4

But the non-zero-sum conceptions of politics is not automatically assured by the establishment of constitutional democratic regimes and the promulgation of constitutions. Many constitutional democratic regimes, such as those in Central Europe in the 1930s and the United States during the Civil War, have foundered exactly because they were unable to incorporate the symbols and themes of protest and different sectors of the population into their central framework.

The non-zero-sum notion of politics and the related capacity to incorporate themes and symbols of protest are contingent on specific social conditions. Some of these are, of course, closely connected to those that have been analyzed in great detail in the extensive literature dealing with the continuity of democratic regimes.[3] The three most important have been, first, the potential for many different actors to have enough resources to enter and continue the political game, that is, to distribute resources and power in society; second, the promulgation of the rules of the game and of adherence to them; and, third, the concomitant construction of public spheres.

The most important concrete conditions within the first set is the non-monopolization by any group or sector of the major resources and sources of power in the society. That is, a multiplicity of centers of power must exist and be continually reproduced, have control over resources potentially beyond the reach of the political powers (whether absolutist, republican, or revolutionary communitarian), but at the same time have potential access to the centers of their respective societies.

Originally it was the relationship between the rulers (kings) and rising bourgeois and autonomous intellectual and professional forces of early modern societies that was crucial in this respect. Later the configuration changed, with the relations between capitalists and workers becoming central. Still later, from about the middle or the end of the nineteenth century, public-private bureaucratic organizations have become yet another component of this configuration.

The development of such multiple centers of power has been influenced by the tempo and continuity of economic development, the relations and balance of power among the different economic groups and between them and the center, and the extent of economic gaps between various sectors of the population and the political center. In this context that economic processes do not allow monopolies of resources or the exclusion of groups from access to them and to positions of power is of crucial importance.

It is not, however, just the existence of multiple social sectors, of centers of power autonomous from the state, that is of crucial importance for the foundation and continuous functioning of constitutional democratic institutions. The second set of crucial conditions is the continual development of autonomous access of these groups to the central political arena, not only in the purely formal sense of suffrage but also in terms of the possibility of actual participation in the central political arena and/or of influence on it, and the concomitant acceptance by the major political actors of the rules of the game put forth in this arena.

Such acceptance is greatly reinforced by the third crucial set of conditions—namely, the existence and continual functioning of public, institutional arenas that serve as links between those sectors and the political arena, above all the development of autonomous public arenas that are not embedded either in the state or within fixed ascriptive or corporate frameworks of any sectors of the society and are not controlled by the state but have autonomous access to the political arena and through which there flows politically relevant information. It is the prevalence of these public arenas and the continual flow within them of open communication and information that are crucially important in facilitating the autonomous access of major social sectors to the political arena. These sectors, continually engaged in the political arena, are consequently able to call for the accountability of the rulers.

5

The importance of these structural conditions for the relatively successful, continual functioning of constitutional democratic regimes has been amply illustrated in the literature, but in themselves they are not sufficient to assure this functioning. That is highly dependent on the development and reproduction or continuity within the politically active sectors of society of the non-zero-sum conception of politics. It is true that the prevalence of these structural conditions contributes to the development and continuity of this conception, but it neither generates it nor assures its continual development.

It is the major argument of my analysis that these structural conditions—the distribution of power in society, the access of different groups to the center, the acceptance by them of the rules of the game promulgated in the center, and the construction of public spheres—contribute greatly to the development of the non-zero-sum conception of politics and to continuity of constitutional democratic regimes only—or mainly—insofar as they develop in tandem with the construction and reconstruction or reproduction of the linkages of trust among various sectors of the society and between them and the broader institutional arenas, of trust in the macro-societal order as symbolized in its centers and institutions.

By trust I mean the following, quoting Claus Offe:

Trust is the *belief* that others will do certain things or refrain from doing certain things. The truster knows that the action of the trusted others will have consequences for his own welfare, and that for this reason there is a *risk* involved in trusting. Trust is a reflectively fallible ex ante guess. It follows the logic: "I know it *can* happen, yet I believe it *won't happen*," with "it" being some undesired event caused by the trusted.

The dynamics of trust-building can be represented on the time axis. Trust, once its necessary and sufficient conditions are met, is a steady state capable of reproducing itself. What is associated with this steady state is a perception of predictability, consistency, robustness concerning the behavior of relevant others. . . . He who has always remained faithful to shared beliefs and values and performed competently will continue to do so in the future—at least in the absence of irritating events and perceptions that lead the actor to reconsider whom to trust, to what extent to trust, and in what respects. In the absence of such irritating events, a trust relation is self-enforcing.[4]

Offe also explains:

But trust is inherently fragile. Trust does indeed constitute a precondition for the continuity of any long-range social interactions but at the same time it is not naturally given but continually constructed and reconstructed—and hence also potentially fragile. It is fragile first of all because it entails a strong element of uncertainty, of risk. This risk results to follow Margaret Levi "from the fact that the truster is *unable to make sure* or *know for certain* that the other person(s) will actually act in the way preferred by the truster. The means by which he might be able to make this sure—coercive *power*, economic resources to be employed as *incentives*, and certain *knowledge* derived from direct observation or tested causal theories—are not at the disposal of the truster.[5]

The fragility of trust is exacerbated in any broader institutional setting because the conditions that make for maintenance of trust are best met in relatively limited ranges of social activities or interaction, such as in family or kinship groups in which social interaction is regulated according to primordial and/or particularistic criteria. Such limited ranges of interaction seem to constitute the necessary minimal conditions for the initial development of trust, even if they may not be enough to guarantee its continuity, even in these settings. At the same time, however, these very conditions may be inimical to the development of those resources and activities needed for broader institutional creativity and for the construction of broader institutional complexes based on more variegated orientations. The very conditions that generate resources for broader complex institution building also tend to undermine the simple settings of potential trust as they exist within the family and kinship groups or in small communities. The possibility of the institutionalization of such broad institutional complexes is above all dependent on the effective extension of the range of trust, its symbols and normative obligations, beyond the narrow minimal scope of primordial units. Such extension is found, for example, in the depiction of rulers as "fathers" of their countries.[6]

But the extension of trust and its interweaving within broader institutional settings necessarily entails possible conflicts with regard to the criteria of allocation of resources. These are closely related to the differences between the criteria of allocation in small, primary settings and those set from different centers derived from broader, universalistic criteria, often as for instance in the Axial civilizations. In all Axial civilizations, such permeating from the center into the family units (and into the periphery in general) and the consequent connection to family and local settings were legitimized in terms of some universalistic principle, such as the notion of sovereignty of God in the monotheistic religions, promoted by the center, thus necessarily generating potential tensions among the bearers of these different criteria.

This problematique of trust becomes even more fully exacerbated in constitutional democratic regimes. As Mark Warren, from Georgetown University, has put it (private correspondence):

> The paradox here is that the relationship between democracy and trust is complex: conflicts indicate that trust is absent and probably inappropriate, and yet any non-zero-sum way of addressing the conflict requires that (a) the conflict be contained by other relationships (and institutions) that include trust; and (b) the process of conflict resolution itself generates trust. In the absence of these possibilities, democracy is at best fragile.

6

Such possibilities develop in modern constitutional democratic regimes insofar as structural conditions of democracy analyzed in the literature—that is, the distribution of power in society, the access of different groups to the center and the acceptance by them of the rules of the game promoted by the center, and the construction of public spheres—are combined with the formation of relatively stable institutional frameworks that enable, first, the participation of the major active sectors of society in formulating and interpreting the rules of the political game, and, second, that assure their continual attachment to the political and national collectivities and identification with them. Such development in turn depends on the continual reconfiguration of several closely interrelated conditions or factors. One central factor that has been neglected in the literature—or at least in its relation to the development of trust of non-zero-sum game conceptions of politics and of the continuity of constitutional democratic regimes—is the construction of collective identity.

The construction of collective identity is closely related to that of trust, above all because it entails the social construction of boundaries of collectivities, the definition of "similarity," and hence also of solidarity, among the members of the collectivity as against the strangeness, the differences, or the distinctiveness of the other or others. But while the construction of collective identity constitutes one of the social processes or mechanisms that may facilitate trust in both micro- and macrosettings, yet at the same time, because it raises the fragility of trust to a new level, it also entails the possibility of social conflicts and the breakdown of trust. Fragility is inher-

ent in most macrosocietal settings because of the multiplicity of the criteria according to which collective identity is constituted and the close relation of such codes to the allocation of resources. Hence it is the modes of
construction of collective identity as they are connected with the construction of the broader political community that are of crucial importance in
the construction and reproduction of trust.

7

Let me illustrate this point by a brief look at some aspects of the European
experience, especially at the importance of the relations among, on the one
hand, primordial, civil, whether religious or secular, and universalistic components in the construction of collective identities and, on the other hand,
the construction of macrosocietal trust. I shall start by examining one aspect that has been often emphasized in the literature—namely, the impact
in the continual institutionalization of the constitutional, later constitutional democratic, regimes, or on their breakdown in Europe from the
early nineteenth century, of the extent to which there occurred a relatively
long-term temporal convergence between crystallization of the modern
state and of the boundaries of collectivities and the extent to which the
conception of accountability of rulers to the body of citizens were institutionalized before the processes of political democratization and mobilization developed. Such temporal sequence was, as has been well researched,
on the whole conducive to the development, institutionalization, and continuity of constitutional regimes. But, as the case of France and especially
of Spain attest, this temporal sequence was not in itself enough to assure
continuity. Here of great importance was the mode of construction of the
symbolic boundaries of the emerging modern collectivities, of their collective identity, and above all of the ways in which primordial, ethnic, or national, sacred, civil, and universalistic orientations were a part of them. Of
special significance in this connection has been the extent to which the primordial, the civil, and the universalistic dimensions or components of collective identity became interwoven in different societies, and especially the
extent to which in the experience of those societies none of these dimensions was totally absolutized or set up by their respective bearers against
the other dimensions.

In all modern European societies there developed a continual tension
between the primordial components of identity, reconstructed in modern

terms as nationalism and ethnicity, and the various sacred, more traditional religious or secular, universalistic, and civil components. The most important aspect of this development, from the point of view of the continuity or breakdown of constitutional regimes, has been the mode in which the secular, universalistic, and civic components of collective identity were combined not only with the older religious ones but also with very strong primordial ones that became redefined and reconstituted in the course of modernization. The way these different components interrelated greatly influenced the fate of constitutional democratic reforms that developed in European societies.

These interrelationships and their influence on the legitimation of their respective regimes were very closely related, as Seymour Martin Lipset and Stein Rokkan have shown,[7] to the resolution of religious conflicts attendant on the Reformation and Counter-Reformation. They were also closely related to the ways in which the secular components of the Enlightenment meshed with the various religious and civic components predominant in their respective societies, as the relations among the political, national, and religious collectivities were constructed.

One resolution of the religious issue, which developed mostly in Counter-Reformation Catholic countries, especially Spain, Portugal, and Italian states and later in a different mode in Poland, was characterized by the repression of religious minorities and by the incorporation of the Catholic symbols as the exclusive symbols and institutional frameworks of the national collectivity and the consequent subsumption of civil components under rigid religious ones. Attendant institutional arrangements and entitlements included the monopolization by the church of marriage laws and the vesting of these institutions with de facto veto power over constitutional arrangements.

The other mode of resolution of religious and cultural conflicts developed in France and above all in Germany. Here the religious question (the divide between Catholics and Protestants, or between traditional religious groups and secularists) constituted a continuous focus of political division and struggle around the construction of the symbols of collective identity and of the scope of autonomous spaces for religious groups in such arenas as education or marriage.

In Germany the confessional split between the Catholic and the Protestant states (formerly autonomous kingdoms or principalities), all of which were rooted in the post-Reformation principle of *cuius regio eius religio*—with the modern imperial center attempting especially under Otto von Bismarck to wage an ultimately unsuccessful *Kulturkampf* against the Catholics—exacerbated the political tensions between these religious groups and was not conducive to the development of a multifaceted pattern of collective consciousness.

Both these resolutions were in marked contrast to those that developed in Protestant countries in which, indeed, constitutional regimes were successfully institutionalized. In these Protestant countries the relative depoliticization of the religious cleavages often caused the totalistic vision, inherent in the extreme Protestant sects, to fail. While totalistic orientations weakened, the more egalitarian and individualistic components in Protestant groups grew strong.

This partial depoliticization of political cleavages took place within the Protestant countries in different ways. One pattern developed in Lutheran countries, especially in Scandinavia, where it was characterized by a relatively homogeneous ethnic and religious identity. Here depoliticization took the paradoxical form of the establishment of a Lutheran State Church that became closely connected with the State and one of the major socializing agencies of the modern State. In England, Holland, and Switzerland, which were characterized by religious and—to various degrees—ethnic heterogeneity, such depoliticization developed a higher degree of pluralism and of autonomy of civil society. In the latter countries the victory of Protestantism also gave rise to the partial, but only partial, depoliticization of religious groups, including sectarian Protestant groups, and it was closely connected with the gradual—indeed very gradual—development of relative toleration toward other Christian (including Protestant sectarian) religious groups.

Thus John Stephans is indeed correct in emphasizing the importance of—especially Protestant—sectarianism for the development of democracy, but significantly it is above all within Protestantism that strong tendencies to independent autonomous sectarianism developed.[8] This was due not just to the Protestant belief system but rather to the interweaving of this system with the structure of political and religious elites and their relations to broader sectors of society—to the strong elective affinities between Protestant, especially radical Protestant, beliefs and the openness and accountability of elites. True enough, strong totalistic tendencies developed within such Protestant sects, as was the case in Calvin's Geneva and in many of the Dutch and American Calvinist sects. But when such tendencies were undermined they could generate—in contrast to the Catholic countries—strong constitutional and democratic tendencies.[9]

8

These patterns of resolution of the religious conflict were closely related to the patterns of the development of collective identity in various European countries.

In the Scandinavian countries the close connection of State and Church gave rise to collective identities in which religious, political, and national elements, with strong Enlightenment components, became strongly interwoven, at the same time taking religious issues out of the central political arena. In these countries, and in England, Holland, and Switzerland, the emergence of collective identity was characterized by the close connections of the primordial and religious components with the civil and universalistic components without the former being denied, allowing a relatively wide scope for pluralistic arrangements. In these countries there developed a relatively successful—even if never bereft of tension—combination of primordial and territorial, statist conceptions and symbols of collective identity, together with strong centers within which representative institutions played an important part.

In all these countries confrontations between the secular orientations of the Enlightenment, which often contained strong deistic orientations, and the strong religious orientation of various Protestant sects were muted. In Scandinavia the Enlightenment was embued with pietistic orientations, and the religious and secular components were closely connected.

In those societies and in Central Europe, above all in Germany, and in most countries of Southern and Central Europe, the construction of the collective identities of the modern nation-state was marked by continual confrontations between the primordial and the civil and universalistic components and as well as between traditional religious and modern universalistic components. In these countries there developed a stronger tendency to crises and breakdowns of different types of constitutional arrangements. The tension between the bearers of the primordial and of civil and universalistic components of collective identities, rooted in the premises of the Enlightenment and often formulated in Jacobin mode, gave rise to movements that emphasized the exclusiveness and absolutization of the primordial and/or of the universalistic components of the new collective consciousness. In the more authoritarian regimes, such primordial components were promulgated in traditional terms, and in totalitarian, fascist, or national socialist movements, in strongly racist terms, while the universalistic orientations were promulgated by various leftist Jacobin movements.

In this context of crucial importance has been the extent to which various groups—such as the Church and aristocratic, oligarchic, military, or revolutionary social groups—were forbidden to have a veto over the symbols of collective boundaries. In such cases neither the religious nor the revolutionary symbols or orientations became the foci of continuous contention. Needless to say, tensions among these orientations and their bearers were constant, but they were usually resolved within the framework of the new states and modern constitutional institutions. Or, in other words, in these societies the religious and Jacobin revolutionary orientations or symbols tended to become interwoven with one another and with the more primordial and civil ones, and the more totalistic and absolutist dimensions of each diminished.

France constitutes a very important—probably the most important—illustration of the problems arising out of continual confrontations between Jacobin and traditional components in the legitimation of modern regimes, even within the framework of relatively continuous polity and collective identity and boundaries. Above all, France illustrates that under such conditions, pluralistic tendencies and arrangements do not develop easily. The weakness of their development is closely related to the consequent turbulence in the institutions of constitutional democratic regimes.

9

It is thus the construction of multifaceted collective identity that constitutes an important condition for the development of frameworks of mutual trust among the different sectors of society. Different modes of construction in different European societies have greatly influenced the development within them of pluralistic tendencies manifest in their relations to minorities. The mode of incorporation of Jews into different European societies is highly indicative of these relations.

In those societies in which the primordial components were relatively successfully interwoven with the civil and universalistic components in the construction of collective identity—as was to some extent the case in England, Holland, and the Scandinavian countries—Jews were allowed a relatively wide scope for integration into society. But in those societies in which there were strong tensions among the primordial, civil, and religious and secular, universalistic components—as was the case in Central Europe, above all in Germany and in many social movements in Western Europe—

the Jewish experience went in a different direction. In these societies there was a strong negative emphasis on the primordial components central to Jewish collective identity that led to the Jews' being denied the possibility of incorporation into the modern nation-state.[10] These themes were increasingly promoted by modern antisemitic movements that stressed the unique character of the Jews, defined them as an alien caste or race, and argued their inability to assimilate fully into the respective European societies. These tendencies ultimately led to the Holocaust, the epitome of modern barbarism.[11]

10

But the construction of collective identity does not, of course, take place in an institutional vacuum. It has been connected in Europe—and beyond Europe—to specific institutional conditions in addition to those emphasized in the literature on democracy. The most important of these have been the flexibility of the centers, the mutual openness of elites, and their relations to broader social strata. Without going into a detailed analysis, suffice it to point out here that there developed in Europe, and later in other societies, a close elective affinity between the absolutizing types of collective identity and various types of absolutist regimes and rigid centers, and between the multifaceted pattern of collective identity in which the primordial, civil, and sacred components were continually interwoven with the development of relatively open and flexible centers and of mutual openings between various strata. The concomitant development of relatively strong states, relatively open or multifaceted modes of collective identity, and autonomous access of major strata to the center was of crucial importance in making possible the participation of major social actors in the national political framework, in the formulation and interpretation of the rules of the political game, and in their ability to call for the accountability of rulers. These conditions facilitated the development of a distinct type of civil society—a society that was to a large extent autonomous *from* the state but at the same time autonomous *in* the state and had an autonomous access to the state and participated in formulating the rules of the political game. The development of this type of civil society has reinforced the relative commitment of the constituent groups of the major political actors, historically first the upper and middle classes, later the working class—as well as of the major elites—to the broad political community, to the center, and to the major representative institutions. These conditions influenced also the extent to which the center and these institutions were viewed, as was the case for instance in seventeenth- and eighteenth-century Poland, as arenas for extracting resources for the major groups, but also as arenas that entailed obligation for the implementation of some common good.

It is insofar as the structural conditions emphasized in the literature on democracy—dispersion of the centers of power in a society and the possibility of their access to the center, promulgation of rules of the game, and construction of public spheres—develop in conjunction with flexibility of centers, with open relations among elites and between them and broader strata, and with multifaceted conceptions of collective identity that there emerges among the major political actors a non-zero-sum conception of the political game.

The central focus of these conditions has been the continual construction and reconstruction of the relations between the solidarity and trust generated in various sectors of society and of societal trust in the broader frameworks as symbolized in its center. Some recent analyses of the breakdown of the Weimar republic are of great interest from the point of view of this discussion. These new analyses, as against older theories that stressed the depoliticization and pauperization of the middle classes and consequent development of a shapeless mass society, have shown that it was not necessarily the absence of civil society or just a faint development thereof, but rather the dissociation among different organized sectors and between them and the center, their basic attitudes to the center, the weakness of the interlinking arenas and of mutual trust among them and between them and center that have been of crucial importance. Of special significance in breaking down trust was the rift between the older elites, which were the mainstay of imperial business, as against the social democratic and liberal elites and the misunderstanding by the former of the intensity of the impact of war and the economic situation.[12]

In Eastern and Southern Europe the weakness of relatively autonomous sectors of civil society and of relations of trust among them and between them and the center was very important in shaping the fate of constitutional regimes. In many of these countries—Spain, Portugal, Greece, to some extent Italy, in most of the countries in Eastern Europe with the exception of Czechoslovakia, which became independent after the First World War—the combination of this weakness, together with strong dissociation between them and the state, was closely related to the breakdown of constitutional regimes. With the partial exception of Italy, given the relatively low and uneven economic development and relatively low level of social mobilization, this breakdown gave rise mostly to autocratic and fascist regimes, not to fully totalitarian ones.[13]

II

Let me illustrate the importance of the various conditions mentioned above for the construction of trust by a very brief analysis of the reasons for the failure of the fascist movements to seize power, despite their relative strength, in the Scandinavian countries in the 1930s. I shall follow here a recent study by Erik Lindström[14] that in a sense applies Werner Sombart's question to fascism in Scandinavia. Lindström asks why, despite economic depression, widespread dissatisfaction among lower-middle groups, and the rudiments of fascist movements and sentiments, these movements were not successful.

Lindström's analysis proceeds on two levels. On the first he stresses that the major political parties succeeded in preventing the ideological and organizational success of the fascist movement. Of special importance here were the incorporation of rightist symbols or slogans by the more conservative parties, thus preempting them politically, and the ability of all organized political parties and economic groups to incorporate the highly mobilized masses.

At the same time, on the political-coalitional level, the Crisis Agreement, which upheld the democratic framework and the fight against fascist movements, and coalitions between conservative and social democratic parties prevented the development of party cleavages and political ruptures, which were instrumental in the breakdown of parliamentary regimes in Germany, Italy, and Central and Eastern Europe.

On the second level of analysis, Lindström shows that the establishment of such coalitions, above all in the Crisis Agreement, was not due just to clever party politics but also to basic conceptions of the political realm, to a conscious commitment by the various elites to the parliamentary constitutional system, to a long tradition of a unified polity, and to the absence of religious cleavages. Significantly enough, this commitment was shared by all the parties—peasant, conservative, and (reformist) social democratic, which at the same time also shared a strong element of class consciousness. But, in line with tradition and the experience of the Scandinavian estate systems, this class consciousness, although by definition containing antagonistic elements, was nevertheless based on participation in a common center and on a certain commitment to it.

Of special importance in the Scandinavian context was also the fact that the basic components of collective identity—the universalistic, the civil, and the primordial components of modern collective consciousness—became closely interwoven in these countries without leading to the absolutization of any one of them, especially the primordial and/or the sacral components or to their mutual exclusion.

In this context it is very interesting to analyze the fate of folkist, potentially fascist themes in Scandinavian countries. Just as in the potentially militant class consciousness in socialist movements, a very strong emphasis on romantic folkist themes, much like those that developed in German nationalist and later national socialist groups, was taken up by conservative and social democratic groups alike. This emphasis was incorporated into the general symbols of collective identity promoted by the parliamentary state. Various folk activities, such as the construction of folk homes, were undertaken by conservative parties, and later by social democratic parties and/or state agencies.

Indeed the Scandinavian countries, especially Sweden, shared some of the characteristics that were often singled out as the "causes" of Germany's turn to national socialism. The most important of these were strong corporate traditions, the predominance of landed and industrial elites, the weakness of the liberal bourgeoisie, late modern capitalist and industrial development, and strong conformist traditions. Yet, despite these similarities, fascist movements did not take over in Scandinavia. There was, of course, one important difference between the class structure of Scandinavian countries and class structure in continental Europe: a strong independent peasantry and the concomitant relative weakness of feudal traditions. But these cannot be understood without taking into account the specific structure of the Swedish state and the role of a strong political national community in the construction of its collective identity. These factors, above all, have to be taken into account in explaining both the lack of success of the fascist movements and the mode of political participation of the working classes in the Scandinavian states.

Certain aspects of the Scandinavian historical experience are of special importance in this context.[15] First is the continuity of the political center in most of these countries, especially in Sweden and Denmark. Second is the very strong tradition of participation by different classes, through assemblies of estates, in the center, combined with acceptance of the predominance of the center. This predominance was strongly emphasized during periods of absolutism, when the power of the estates was weakened, but the autonomous place of the estates was never obliterated. Third is the relatively early establishment, with the partial exception of Finland, of national unity without religious cleavages. This unity even developed in Norway, which was long under Swedish or Danish domination. Fourth is the depoliticization of the clergy, which took place early in the Reformation, combined with a strong activist, this-worldly orientation.

These developments in the Scandinavian countries were closely related to relatively strong family and regional cohesion, not segregated from the centers but linked to them and to one another through a variety of cultural, religious, educational, and political channels and through the activities of the political, cultural, and social elites. These activities were characterized by strong tendencies to autonomy but were at the time highly oriented to the center and to some extent regulated by the state.

This last tendency was closely related to the paradoxical way in which the general European tendency to confrontation between state and society developed in these countries. It would be only a slight exaggeration to suggest that among all the democratic European political polities, this distinction was weakest in the Scandinavian countries—perhaps above all in Sweden— and the democratic state, and earlier the absolutist state, was often seen as coterminous with society. This situation was connected with the paradoxical combination of strong commitment to the center and strong class consciousness, based on the implicit assumption that the center constitutes the proper arena for working out different visions and the concomitant reconstruction of society according to class values.

This combination was evident in the development of strong social democratic and agrarian parties alike. These parties shared, with the more bourgeois parties, a strong political class consciousness that by its very nature contained substantial elements of contention. At the same time, this class consciousness, particularly in its socialist version, was—in Marxist nomenclature—rather reformist. For most of their history these parties accepted the tenets of constitutional democracy and the legitimacy of the constitutional center.

1 2

The importance of the connection between the multifaceted pattern of collective identities and the construction of macrosocietal trust as it developed in different countries in Europe was rooted in the problems of the extension of trust as they crystallized in the framework of Axial civilizations. In all these civilizations there developed a tension between the primordial bases of trust and their universalistic premises. The way these tensions were resolved played an important role in the institutional dynamics of these societies. Of special importance in the resolution of tensions was the development of institutional frameworks such as the law of contracts and of relatively independent legal and political institutions based on universalistic criteria that could uphold the continual extension of trust based on these criteria, ultimately providing for the possibility of development of non-zero-sum conceptions of economic and political interaction.

From this point of view it might be of great interest to compare, even if very briefly, the connections between the construction of trust in relation to collective identity and institutional dynamics in Japan—a non-Axial civilization that developed a successful modern capitalist constitutional regime, and after the Second World War, a constitutional democratic regime. From the point of view of this analysis the great puzzle of modern Japanese society is how a modern constitutional, later democratic polity, and a successful modern capitalist economy, could develop in a society in which trust based on universalistic criteria has not developed. One clue lies in the specific mode of the construction of Japanese collective identity and in the closely related characteristics of the construction of trust in Japanese society.

As we have seen above, in contrast to what happened in the Axial civilizations, the construction of Japanese collective identity involved the denial of the relevance of universalistic ideologies in the Confucian and Buddhist ones, promulgated by the bearers of the Axial civilizations, in relation to the primordial components and the concomitant construction of this consciousness or identity in terms of sacral liturgical community and of the emphasis or on the uniqueness of the Japanese collectivity or nation.

The success of Japanese elites in denying universalistic components of the Axial age civilization that were continually impinging on them was closely related to their basic characteristics. The most important of these was the embedment of elites and major coalitions in groups and settings or contexts that were defined mainly in primordial, ascriptive, sacral, and often hierarchial terms, and much less in terms of specialized function or universalistic criteria.[16]

Linked to this characteristic was the relative weakness of autonomous cultural elites. True, many cultural or religious specialists—priests, monks, scholars, and the like—participated in elite coalitions, but with very few exceptions their participation was based on primordial and social attributes and on criteria of achievement and social obligations to different particularistic contexts in which these coalitions were structured and not on any autonomous criteria rooted in or related to the arenas in which they were active. These arenas—cultural, religious, economic—were themselves ultimately defined in primordial-sacral and not in universalistic or transcendental terms. It was these elites, in continual interaction with the broader strata, that generated in Japan the continual construction and extension of a very distinct pattern of generalized trust.

The distinctive characteristic of Japanese civilization important for this analysis has been the fact that its larger framework was based on a continuous extension of trust, symbolized primordial kinship terms, from the family to broader institutional formations. In other words, the permeation of the basic family units and the mobilization of family resources by broader institutional formations, by the center, was legitimized in kinship terms. The extension of familial trust has been, in Japan, couched in broader, generalized kinship terms and symbols, with strong expressive components, and not in terms of criteria beyond such kinship symbols. This generalized particularistic trust, which is close to but not identical with what Robert Bellah has defined as generalized particularism,[17] is not confided to narrow settings but is generalized over many different settings or situations. It is a generalized trust defined in broad, continually changing, particularistic terms. Such generalization of trust is not promulgated in universalistic, but in particularistic terms and is made possible by the fact that it is effected by the continual movement among different particularistic contexts, defined in sacral-primordial and civil terms.

As against this, in all the Axial civilizations permeation by the center of the family units, and of the periphery in general, was legitimized in terms of universalistic principles. Accordingly, there developed a break and potential confrontation between trust defined in primordial terms and the claims of universalistic principles. In all these civilizations the interweaving of the primordial with the universalistic components of collective identity constituted a potential point of contention. The Confucian controversy over the relative priority of filial piety as against loyalty to one's lord—a controversy that developed in all Axial civilizations—is but one illustration. In these civilizations such confrontations were effected, as was the permeation of the center into the periphery and into the various familial settings, by various autonomous cultural and political elites and influentials, often organized in various sects and heterodoxies, who, in their interaction with broader sectors of the society, also were the most active in the ideological reconstruction of centers, collectivities, and institutional formations and in their attendant struggles.

In contrast, the extension of trust from the family units to broader settings, to the centers, did not entail in Japan confrontation with autonomous elites promoting universalistic principles or confrontation between orthodoxies and heterodoxies. Accordingly the mode of extension of trust generated a distinctive pattern of change and of historical continuity.

This specific mode of the construction and extension of trust that has been so closely related to the construction of collective identity in Japan explains also some of the distinctive characteristics of Japan as a modern polity to which we have referred above. These are, above all, the development of a distinct conception of state and civil society in which both state and civil society are conflated and embedded in the national community and, second, a very strong tendency to nonideological protest. It is these specific modes of extension of trust in Japan and in Axial civilizations that explain, to some extent, the differences among the dynamics of European, American, and Japanese constitutional regimes. In all those societies, the continuity of constitutional regimes has been contingent on the successful extension of trust, on the development of generalized trust. In all these cases this extension has been closely related to the mode of construction of the collective identity, especially to the development of some means of multifaceted interweaving of the various components thereof in different societies. However, the exact mode of this interweaving and relative importance of different components of collective identity have greatly influenced the construction and transferral of trust among different sectors of society and between them and the center, as well as the distinctive characteristics of the democratic regimes that developed in these societies and of their points of vulnerability.

13

We may now bring together the major lines of our analysis of the conditions conducive to the development and continuity of construction and reconstruction of trust, which in its turn facilitates the development and reproduction of a non-zero-sum conception of politics.

The combination of the structural conditions conducive to the development of democratic regimes analyzed in the literature have been crucial in the construction and continual reconstruction of trust in the relations between civil society and the state, and of the linkages between the trust engendered in the various microsettings and the central frameworks and institutions. These conditions include the continual dispersion of centers of power; promotion of rules of the game, and constructions of public spheres with the development of cohesiveness and accessibility of center and of the mutual openings between the major elites and state, and with multifaceted patterns of collective identity. In turn, trust is of crucial importance in facilitating the development of a non-zero-sum conception of politics and in shaping the transformative capacity of constitutional democratic regimes. The failure to reconstruct trust has been conducive to the breakdown of these regimes.

The continual feedback among these conditions tends to give rise to such reconstructions of trust and of a non-zero-sum conception of political groups, first of all because it reinforces the development of an open flow of communication and information within and between different public arenas, and between them and broader sector of the society and the centers. This continual flow is crucially important in facilitating the autonomous access of major sectors of society to the political arenas, their engagement within these arenas, and their ability to call for the accountability of rulers.

Second, the continual interweaving of these conditions, albeit in different patterns, reinforces the development and reproduction of those features of the political culture—egalitarianism, political tolerance, participatory and communal forms of decision making—cutting across parochial loyalties that, as Gizelle De Meur and Dirk Berg-Schlosser have shown,[18] have been of crucial importance in countering the fragmentation and polarization that can lead to the breakdown of constitutional regimes and their movement in authoritarian or totalitarian directions.

Third, the interweaving of these conditions influences the extent to which there develop in such regimes chances that at any junction of intensive social change, there will emerge some recombination of the components of collective identity and of different bases of legitimation without total confrontation between different sectors and that some basic orientations to common collective identity or consciousness to a common text referred to by different sectors of the population will continually develop.

Thus the combination of these broad sets of conditions—the crystallization of a common text and the continual reconstruction of public spheres and political organizations, together with the continual dispersion of centers of power and a decoupling of power, wealth, and prestige—enhance the possibility of a continual reinterpretation of the legitimation of the rules of the game in terms that interweave the primordial and cultural or civil orientation without imposing ideological homogeneity on all sectors of the society. These conditions also foster the continual metalegitimation of the rules of the game of constitutional democratic regimes.

14

The preceding analysis has, on the one hand, strongly emphasized a combination of structural and cultural factors as important in shaping the dynamics of modern constitutional and democratic regimes, especially their propensities for transformation or breakdown. On the other hand, the analysis, especially Lindström's analysis of the failure of fascist movements to take over in Scandinavia, has also emphasized the importance of activities of different elites, of, as it were, concrete human action or human agency. The relation between these two sets of factors—both of them strongly emphasized in the literature on democracy—is not simple or direct. One need not assume that the structural and cultural conditions enumerated above necessarily give rise to those types of human agency, of actors, and of activities supportive of continuity of constitutional and constitutional democratic regimes. Conversely, one need not assume that such activities can develop—especially in historical contexts different from those discussed here—only under structural and cultural conditions specified above.

What the preceding analysis does suggest is that the development within the different contexts the conditions analyzed above is highly conducive to the emergence of such actors or activities. It is these conditions that facilitated the concomitant development, to paraphrase the nomenclature of Michael Burton, Richard Gunther, and John Highly, of elite consensus and trust of broader sectors in central governmental and representative institutions.[19] Such elite consensus as related to trust in the central institutions facilitates also the development of some combinations of legitimacy of the regime with relative efficiency in the performance of its central institutions.

But the development of such conditions is not, as we have seen throughout our preceding analysis, given, as it were naturally, in the development of many of these societies.

CHAPTER NINE

TENDENCIES TO DECONSOLIDATION OF DEMOCRACY IN CONTEMPORARY SOCIETIES

I

It is in the nature of constitutional democratic regimes and of their continual development that favorable conditions for their functioning do not automatically assure their continuity or reproduction. True enough, the successful institutionalization of a constitutional democratic regime generates at least some critical reinforcement of such conditions, especially acceptance of the legitimation of the regime and the rules of the political game, a non-zero-sum conception of politics, and of trust in these rules. Yet in any modern constitutional democratic regime there may be processes that undermine these conditions. The very fact that modern societies are continually changing, as well as the basic characteristics of the political process, may undermine initially favorable conditions, and trust may be eroded. Thereby the legitimacy and efficiency of the regime are greatly weakened.

This undermining may take place with respect to all the major conditions analyzed above. First of all, there may develop processes that may change the balance of social, economic, and political forces, thus impairing the plurality of centers of power. Moreover, often the very policies—for example, policies connected with the welfare state—whose initial aim was to weaken semimonopolistic centers of power, can increase the power of the state in its various political and administrative organs to such an extent that they may obliterate independent bases of power. The bureaucratization of all areas of social life, including political arenas, has created one such possibility, and the specter of bureaucratization has haunted modern social discourse, as Alexis de Tocqueville, Karl Marx, and Max Weber, attest. The force of this specter has, of course, been reinforced by the development of the totalitarian regimes.

Yet another possibility of such overconcentration of power relates to one of the central nerves of the democratic process—the production and distribution of information and of access to information, the growing professionalism and "technocratization" of knowledge and information relevant to the political process, and the possibility that such knowledge will be presented by many experts and political leaders as beyond the ability of the broader sectors of society to comprehend it. This process may lead to political apathy and withdrawal from political participation. The growing power of the media may, as has been so often stressed, reinforce these trends. Such developments may also undermine the balance within the political arena itself, especially between different branches of the government, above all increasing the power of the executive branch.

Second, the autonomy and distinctiveness of different elites and of the center, as well as of the major public arenas, may be undermined, especially in situations of intensive change. In these situations various autonomous sectors of civil society as well as public arenas may become eroded, and there may develop impediments to restructuring the relations between civil society and the state. These impediments may develop because whenever attempts were made to redefine the boundaries of the political, as for instance in the demands for the extension of suffrage, there arose a tension between, on the one hand, the adherence to the existing rules of the game and the balance between the state and civil society and, on the other hand, the newly emerging social forces and their demands—in a word, between the constitutional and democratic dimensions of these regimes. Within all these sectors, old and new alike, there may develop tendencies to represent narrow corporate or ascriptive sectors, weakening whatever initial acceptance of the newly emerging common frameworks and centers existed among the older, existing power holders. Each group may perceive the others as representing only narrow interests, and no group really cares about the common good.

Among those demanding the redefinition of the realm of the political, the suspicion tends to arise that the existing representative institutions serve only to uphold various concrete, diverse interests, and not some vision of common good. The new contending groups tend to promulgate the importance of different sets of rights, especially those promoting equality against what seem to them to be very narrow interests of a small club to which only members of the upper classes can de jure or de facto be admitted. This accusation was, of course, leveled by many critics, especially from the left, of the liberal democratic regimes, epitomized in Anatole France's famous dictum that the beggar sleeping under the bridge has the same equal rights as the wealthy bourgeois. Indeed, it was often the existing power holders and various strong semimonopolistic, oligarchic groups that tended to uphold different rights, especially the right of property, which assured, in that situation, their standing against newly emerging groups. But at the same time the older groups tended to claim they were the representatives of the common good, as against the newcomers who promulgated only their narrow, egoistical—even if relatively widespread—interests and who wanted to use the representative institutions to promote those interests.

The reconstruction of the state and of civil society that takes place in such situations entails almost by definition a confrontation between the basic conceptions of democracy, especially between the constitutional and different participatory conceptions. It entails also claims for the redefinition of the common good, of the general will, as well as of rights and entitlements. It is all these possibilities that epitomize the paradox of the transformability of the modern constitutional regimes—the crux of which lies, as we have seen, in the fact that any such transformation entails some metalegitimations beyond the (existing) rules of the game and their legitimation but at the same time must be effected within the framework of democratic constitutional regimes, through these very institutions.

2

The erosion and weakening of these autonomous arenas and the concomitant erosion or breakdown of trust may take place not only through the impact of broad social or economic processes on these arenas but also from within the very political process that takes place in all modern regimes, including constitutional democratic regimes. Erosion may occur in the process of leadership selection. Only those who are willing to enter political contests may be selected, and those who are willing to run who may not command the trust and the respect of broader sectors of the population. Or these people may indulge or abuse the privileges of their offices. Or their character may deter people who do command respect from entering the political arena. And there will be those who are unwilling to expose their private lives to scrutiny, which seems to be endemic to new conceptions of public-private relations.

Concomitantly the very processes of democratization may bring with them the demand for immediate, short-term results, with less attention to long-range problems and to populist claims, with less consideration for the long-range aggregation of political needs. An additional aspect is that the capacity for decision making may be overburdened by the political process or, as has been claimed in the contemporary welfare state, demands for resources may overburden the state.[1]

3

Many processes weakening autonomous public arenas and leading to the potential erosion of trust in the institutional frameworks of constitutional democratic regimes have developed in contemporary societies in close relation to broad and intensive process of change. The most important among these have been, first, changes in the international systems and shifts of hegemonies within them, above all the weakening of Western hegemonies; second, the development, throughout the world, but especially in non-Western societies, of a series of highly destabilizing processes connected with economic and cultural globalization; third, the exhaustion of the Cold War's ideological confrontations, culminating in the disintegration of the Soviet regime; fourth, ideological and institutional developments in Western societies in what has been often designated as a postmodern—and multicultural and mainly, although not only, in non-Western societies in fundamentalist[2]—direction.

All these developments gave rise to a rather paradoxical situation in societies all over the world. On the one hand there developed a continual strengthening of the "technocratic" rational, secular policies, in arenas such as education and family planning. But on the other hand these policies were not able to cope adequately with most of these new problems attendant on the processes analyzed above. All these processes became closely connected with the weakening or transformation of the basic ideological and institutional premises of the hitherto prevailing model of the modern nation-state, giving rise in many parts of the world to, on the one hand, strong tendencies to multiculturalism and, on the other hand, growing ethnic, national, and religious conflicts.

4

The impact of these global processes was initially most visible within the societies of Asia, Latin America, and Africa. But at the same time new developments and discourses in Western societies have greatly transformed the initial model of modernity in what has often been designated as postmodern direction and have undermined the original vision of modern society and the modern nation-state.[3]

These developments signaled rather far-reaching changes in understanding modernity in Western societies, entailing the weakening in Europe of the until-then hegemonic and homogenizing conceptions of modernity as embodied in the modern nation-state and/or revolutionary state and in the strength of the secular components in the construction of collective identities as they developed—or were perceived as having developed—in the West. In the United States these changes gathered momentum in the 1960s in the context of the weakening of the religious components in the American public sphere and the consciousness and seemingly successful institutionalization of what was seen by many groups as a godless rational modernity.

On the cultural level these developments entailed first a growing tendency to distinguish between *Zweckrationalität* and *Wertrationalität*, and to the recognition of a great multiplicity of different *Wertrationalitäten*. Cognitive rationality—especially as epitomized in the extreme forms of scientism—has become dethroned, as has also been the idea of the conquest or mastery of the environment, whether of society or of nature. Second, these developments also entailed a very important shift of the utopian orientations predominant in these societies from the construction of modern centers to other arenas.

These developments were closely connected to far-reaching social and cultural changes, signaling the decomposition of the preceding bourgeois culture, with its strong regulative tendencies so forcefully depicted by Max Weber and from different points of view by Norbert Elias and Michael Foucault.[4] There developed a weakening of the former, relatively rigid, homogeneous definition of life patterns, and hence also of the boundaries of family, community, and spatial social organization. Occupational, family, gender, and residential roles have become more and more dissociated from *Staende*, class, and political party frameworks and have regrouped in continuously changing clusters, with relatively weak orientations to such broad frameworks in general and to the societal centers in particular. In the political sphere and in the definition of the citizenship role there have developed tendencies to the redefinition of boundaries of collectivities: to growing dissociation between political centers and the social and cultural collectivities, and to the development of new nuclei of cultural and social identity that transcend existing political and cultural boundaries.

One of the most important institutional changes connected with those tendencies has been the development of various structural, semiliminal enclaves within which new cultural orientations, new modes of the search for meaning—often couched in transcendental terms—tend to be developed and upheld, partially as countercultures, partially as components of new cultural scenes. As a result, new types of social and economic cleavages developed and there was a restructuring of social strata and of the relations between them, as well as from about the 1970s on a new underclass of persons presumably unemployed in the age of globalization of the technological media.

The combinations of these changes in the symbolic definition of different arenas of social life and of structural changes gave rise to a growing diversification of the process of strata formation, to the development of a very diversified crisscross of political, sectorial, and occupational formations. Thus, instead of the situation characteristic of the hitherto modern and industrial society, in which different strata had relatively separate cultural traditions and focused around some broad common political symbols, there has been a continuously greater dissociation among the occupational, cultural, and political spheres of life. Different strata no longer have totally separate different cultures, as before; they tend more and more to participate in common aspects, foci, and arenas of culture in general, and mass culture in particular.

Social strata were continually restructured, transforming relations between them. These developments gave rise to rather complicated differences in life-styles among different status groups and new status sets; new patterns of status or class conflict and struggles; new types of status or class consciousness; and the weakening of overall, especially class or social, ideological orientations in the formation of consciousness. Concomitantly, a new and distinct type of status struggle has developed around the type of welfare benefits distributed by the state. The major themes of class conflicts and struggles have been focused on the state as a distributive, and to a smaller degree regulative, agency. By its very nature, this struggle is occupationally dispersed with but few overall ideological political orientations.

While the concrete economic foci of such status or class struggles have become dispersed among the different demands of various occupational groups, the political and ideological expressions of status consciousness have become less and less focused around economic problems. They became more oriented, even if on the whole in a rather vague and unfocused way, around the center-periphery axis, and/or around the development of distinct styles and patterns of life. There tended also to develop a growing dissociation between high occupational strata and conservative political and social attitudes, creating generations of high executives with cultural, but certainly not economical, leftist views and with an inclination to participate in new permissive enclaves or subcultures. The distinction between left and right generally weakened, as did the close relation between this distinction and the reconstruction of the center that, at least in Europe, was strong. Political discourse became more and more set within a narrow range of issues, combined with a strong tendency to their deideologization, above all in their relation to the center. At the same time there developed new types of social and economic cleavages—on which we have commented above—as well as the new underclass of persons presumably unemployed.

5

This decline of the ideological and institutional premises of the nation state became manifest in a shift in the nature of protest movements that developed from the 1960s on in the development on global scenes of new types of social movements—all of which, however great the difference between them, go beyond the basic premises of the modern nation-state and the revolutionary state.

In most of the European countries it was different "new" social movements such as the women's and the ecology movements which to a high extent developed in close relation to the student and anti-Vietnam war movements of the late sixties and seventies that were most predominant. These stressed growing participation in work, different communal orientations, and the like. Instead of a conflictual-ideological focus on the center and its reconstitution or on the economic conflicts that characterized the earlier, classical social movements of modern and industrial societies, the new movements were oriented to what can be defined as the extension of the systemic range of social life and participation,[5] or by the emphasis on construction of new social spaces as against orientations to the center.

The second major type of new movements which developed in this period and occupied the center stage on the international scene were the fundamentalist and communal religious movements which promulgated strong anti-modern and anti-Western themes. Although these movements developed above all in the non-Western societies—above all in the various Muslim societies—and the communal religious ones in the Hinduist and Buddhist ones, they became also very visible in the West above all in the U.S. where indeed the first modern fundamentalist movements developed. Parallelly there developed, especially in parts of the Balkans and in former republics of the Soviet Union, and in most terrifying ways in Africa, strong particularistic "ethnic" tendencies, movements and conflicts.

All these changes have been connected with a very far-reaching shift away from viewing the political centers of the nation-state as the basic arenas for implementing ontological and social visions. While the political centers of the nation-states continue, even if to a smaller extent, to be the major arena for the distribution of resources, they no longer constitute the major focus of the charismatic dimensions and utopian orientations of various social movements, or of large sectors of the society. This shift was connected with increasing confrontations, on the local scene and global arenas alike, between the original Western conceptions of modernity as embodied in the modern nation-state or revolutionary state and emerging new—local, regional, and transnational—conceptions of collective identity.[6]

Many hitherto "subdued" identities such as local, regional, ethnic, linguistic, came—albeit naturally in a highly reconstructed way—in the centers of their respective societies often contesting the hegemony of the older homogenizing programs or claiming their own autonomous places in the central spaces—be it in educational programs, in public communications and media and very often they are making also far-reaching claims with respect to the redefinition of citizenship and of rights and entitlements connected with it.

The cultural and political homogeneity of the Western European nation-states became also weakened, especially in Western Europe, by the processes leading to growing European units. But these processes generated tendencies to new exclusiveness—either on the local level or on the European level—oriented against Eastern Europe, the Islamic world, and/or the United States. Concomitantly throughout the world there emerged different new diasporas and minorities, often giving rise to ethnic or religious confrontations. These produced a strong emphasis on either multiculturalism and/or fundamentalism and communal nationalism as a possible supplement to the modern nation-state model, or even as a possible replacement.

6

All these global processes may lead to far-reaching changes in the institutional bases of constitutional democracies, indeed to their weakening. Paradoxically these developments take place just when the ideological— especially totalitarian, fascist or communist—opponents of constitutional democracy have disappeared from the scene.

In many constitutional democratic societies—in the United States, Israel, or India, and in a less dramatic way in Europe—these processes have impinged on many of the central nerves of these regimes, producing far-reaching changes. These have included the weakening of parties and of representative institutions as against direct unmediated relations between often amorphous political publics and different political actors, the growth and importance of the media in the political process, and the growing power of the executive, with possible increase in the power of the juridical system as well.

Concomitantly these processes may give rise to or reinforce the deconsolidation of many of the institutional and associational bases of constitutional democratic regimes, to use Larry Diamond's felicitous expression,[7] that is, to the weakening or erosion of components such as the rule of law, freedom from interference by the political authorities in the public and private arenas, and the like. In many contemporary constitutional democratic societies, we witness, as Ralf Dahrendorf pointed out several years ago, the weakening or erosion of the frameworks and bases of civil society.[8] The accumulation of such processes may give rise to distrust and apathy or, at the other end of the continuum, to extremist movements, like the Le Pen movement in France or the numerous ethnic or fundamentalist movements, that have developed around the world.

These tendencies to the weakening of many of the institutional bases of constitutional democracy, especially of autonomous public spheres and of representative institutions, have been reinforced by many aspects of the processes of globalization, especially by attempts to impose, by many international financial institutions as well as transnational corporations, of an extreme market ideology. In Europe these tendencies were reinforced by the fact that within the European Union it was bureaucratic and juridical institutions that were predominant.

At the same time there has developed in many countries a more general trend toward democracies in which elections are indeed held but in which neither the legal institutional guarantees of basic freedoms nor the maintenance of the broader autonomous public are upheld. Such tendencies can be best seen, perhaps, in Latin American countries, and, as has been pointed out by Evelyne Huber, Dietrich Rueschmeyer, and John D. Stephens, they are accompanied by a weakening of participatory democracy.[9] These trends are even more prominent in many countries in Eastern Europe, Asia, and Africa, giving rise to, in Robert Kaplan's expression, "illiberal democracies" or, to use Fareed Zakaria's term, democracies that are not liberal-constitutional ones.[10]

We are witnessing the emergence, both in constitutional democratic and in a great variety of semidemocratic authoritarian regimes throughout the world, of new patterns of political activity closely related to far-reaching changes in the bases of legitimation of these regimes. But these problems are already beyond the scope of this book, although they bear closely on the problem analyzed in it.

NOTES

INTRODUCTION

1. G. O'Donnell, P. Schmitter, and L. Whitehead, eds., *Transitions from Authoritarian Rule: Comparative Perspectives* (Baltimore: Johns Hopkins University Press, 1986), 47–63. See also G. O'Donnell and P. Schmitter, *Transitions from Authoritarian Rule: Tentative Conclusions about Uncertain Democracies* (Baltimore: Johns Hopkins University Press, 1986); J. J. Linz and A. Stepan, *Problems of Democratic Transition and Consolidation* (Baltimore: Johns Hopkins University Press, 1986).

2. L. Diamond, ed., *Political Culture and Democracy in Developing Countries* (Boulder, Colo: Lynne Rienner Publishers, 1993); L. Diamond, J. J. Linz, and S. M. Lipset, eds., *Democracy in Developing Countries*, 4 vols. (Boulder, Colo: Lynne Rienner Publishers, 1989); L. Diamond, J. J. Linz, and S. M. Lipset, eds., *Politics in Developing Countries: Comparing Experiences with Democracy* (Boulder, Colo: Lynne Rienner Publishers, 1990).

CHAPTER I

1. J. A. Schumpeter, *Capitalism, Socialism and Democracy* (London: Unwin University Books, 1974).

2. Very close to Schumpeter's definition, even if not identical with it, is the one proposed by Karl Popper. See K. Popper, "Popper on Democracy: The Open Society and Its Enemies Revisited," *The Economist*, April 23, 1988, 25–28.

3. J. Plamenatz, *Democracy and Illusion: An Examination of Certain Aspects of Modern Democratic Theory* (London: Longman, 1973), chap. 7.

4. Judith Shklar, *Montesquieu* (Oxford: Oxford University Press, 1987); Q. Skinner, *Machiavelli* (New York: Hill and Wang, 1981); Skinner, "The Paradoxes of Political Liberty" "Liberty before Liberalism," and *The Tanner Lectures on Human Values, 1984–85* (Cambridge: Cambridge University Press, 1998); J.G.A. Pocock, *The Machiavellian Moment* (Princeton, N.J.: Princeton University Press, 1975); Pocock, *The Ancient Constitution and the Feudal Law* (Cambridge: Cambridge University Press, 1957); Pocock, *Virtue, Commerce, and History* (Cambridge: Cambridge University Press, 1985); B. Fontana, ed., *The Invention of the Modern Republic* (Cambridge: Cambridge University Press, 1994).

5. For one of the most recent comprehensive expositions of participatory democracy, see C. Pateman, *Participation and Democratic Theory* (Cambridge: Cambridge University Press, 1970).

6. C. McIlwain, *Constitutionalism*, rev. ed. (Ithaca, N.Y.: Cornell University Press, 1947); McIlwain, *The Growth of Political Thought in the West* (New York: Macmillan, 1932).

7. J. L. Talmon, *The Origins of Totalitarian Democracy* (New York: Praeger, 1960). See also J. P. Arnason, "The Theory of Modernity and the Problematic of Democracy," in *Thesis Eleven*, no. 26 (1990): 20–46; C. Lefort, *The Political Forms of Modern Society: Bureaucracy, Democracy and Proletarianism* (Cambridge, Mass.: MIT Press, 1986); Lefort, "On Revolution," in Lefort, *Democracy and Political Theory* (Minneapolis: University of Minnesota Press, 1988), 57–163; *Totalitarian Democracy and After: International Colloquium in Memory of Jacob L. Talmon*, Jerusalem, June 21–24, 1982 (Jerusalem: Israel Academy of Sciences and Humanities and Magnes Press, Hebrew University, 1984), 37–56.

8. E. Shils, "Primordial, Personal, Sacred, and Civil Ties," in Shils, ed., *Center and Periphery: Essays in Macrosociology* (Chicago: University of Chicago Press, 1975), 111–26.

9. On the transformations of liberalism, see John A. Hall, *Liberalism* (London: Paladin, 1987); M. Sandel, ed., *Liberalism and Its Crisis* (Oxford: Blackwell, 1984); *The Relevance of Liberalism*, ed., Institute of International Change (Boulder, Colo.: Westview Press, 1978).

CHAPTER 2

1. See H. G. Koenigsberger, "Riksdag, Parliaments and States General in the Sixteenth and Seventeenth Centuries," in Nils Stjernquist, ed., *The Swedish Riksdag in a Comparative Perspective* (Stockholm: Bank of Sweden Tercentenary Foundation, 1979), 59–79.

2. S. N. Eisenstadt and B. Giesen, "The Construction of Collective Identity," *European Journal of Sociology/Archives Europeennes de Sociologie* 36, no. 1 (1995): 72–102; E. Shils, "Primordial, Personal, Sacred, and Civil Ties."

3. W. Reddy, *The Rise of Market Culture: The Textile Trade and French Society* (Chicago: University of Chicago Press, 1984); Reddy, *Money and Liberty in Modern Europe: A Critique of Historical Understanding* (Cambridge: Cambridge University Press, 1987); H. Breuninger and R. P. Sieferle, eds., *Markt und Macht in der Geschichte* (Stuttgart: Deutsche Verlags-Anstalt, 1995); J. Carrier, *Gifts and Commodities: Exchange and Western Capitalism since 1700* (London: Routledge, 1995); F. Dobbin, *Forging Industrial Policy: The United States, Britain and France in the Railway Age* (New York: Cambridge University Press, 1994); R. Lane, *The Market Experience* (Cambridge: Cambridge University Press, 1991); J. Parry and M. Bloch, eds., *Money and the Morality of Exchange* (Cambridge: Cambridge University Press, 1989).

4. C. Tilly, *Coercion, Capital, and European States, A.D. 990–1990* (Cambridge: Basil Blackwell, 1990); B. Downing, "Constitutionalism, Warfare, and Political Change in Early Modern Europe," *Theory and Society* 17 (1988): 7–56.

5. T. Todorov, *The Morals of History* (Minneapolis: University of Minnesota Press, 1995); Todorov, *The Conquest of America: The Question of the Other* (New York: Harper and Row, 1984).

CHAPTER 3

1. E. Tiryakian, "Three Meta Cultures of Modernity: Christian, Gnostic, Chthonic," *Theory of Culture and Society* 13, no. 1 (1996): 99–118.

2. On the Axial age Civilizations, see S. N. Eisenstadt, "The Axial Age: The Emergence of Transcendental Visions and the Rise of Clerics," *European Journal of Sociology* 23, no. 2 (1952): 294–314; ed., *The Origins and Diversity of Axial-Age Civilizations* (Albany, N.Y.: SUNY Press, 1986).

3. Reddy, *Rise of Market Culture*; Reddy, *Money and Liberty in Modern Europe*; S. Toulmin, *Cosmopolis: The Hidden Agenda of Modernity* (New York: Free Press, 1990); Breuninger and Sieferle, eds., *Markt und Macht in der Geschichte*; Carrier, *Gifts and Commodities*; Dobbin, *Forging Industrial Policy*; Lane, *Market Experience*; Parry and Bloch, eds., *Money and the Morality of Exchange*.

4. Eric Voegelin, *Enlightenment and Revolution*, ed. J. H. Hallowell (Durham, N.C.: Duke University Press, 1975); Voegelin, *The New Science of Politics* (Chicago: University of Chicago Press, 1952); Voegelin, *Die Politischen Religionen* (Munich: Wilhelm Fink Verlag, 1996); Voegelin, *Das Volk Gottes* (Munich: Wilhelm Fink Verlag, 1994); J. LeGoff, ed., *Heresies et societes, civilisations et societes* (Paris: Mouton and Co., 1968); F. Heer, *The Intellectual History of Europe* (Garden City, N.Y.: Doubleday, 1968).

5. C. Bigger, *Kant's Methodology: An Essay in Philosophical Archeology* (Athens, Ohio: Ohio University Press, 1996); Ch. Taylor, *Hegel and the Modern Society* (Cambridge: Cambridge University Press, 1989).

6. A. Salomon, *In Praise of Enlightenment* (Cleveland: World Publishing Co., 1963); Salomon, *The Tyranny of Progress: Reflections on the Origins of Sociology* (New York: Noonday Press, 1955); Toulmin, *Cosmopolis*.

7. S. N. Eisenstadt, *Revolutions and the Transformation of Societies* (New York: Free Press, 1978); Eisenstadt, "Frameworks of the Great Revolutions: Culture, Social Structure, History and Human Agency," *International Social Science Journal*, 133 (1992): 385–401; Eisenstadt, "Transcendental Vision, Center Formation and the Role of Intellectuals," in L. Greenfeld and M. Martin, eds., *Center and Ideas and Institutions* (Chicago: University of Chicago Press, 1980), 96–109.

8. See S. N. Eisenstadt, "Transcendental Vision, Center Formation and the Role of Intellectuals"; Eisenstadt, *Modernization: Protest and Change* (Englewood Cliffs, N.J.: Prentice Hall, 1966); E. Shils, "Primordial, Personal, Sacred, and Civil Ties"; M. Lacey and K. Haakonssen, eds., *A Culture of Rights: The Bill of Rights in Philosophy, Politics, and Law, 1791 and 1991* (Cambridge: Cambridge University Press, 1991).

9. P. Rosanvallon, *Le Sacre du citoyen: Histoire du suffrage universel* (Paris: Editions Gallimard, 1992).

10. M. Walzer, ed., *Regicide and Revolution: Speeches at the Trial of Louis XVI* (London: Cambridge University Press, 1974).

11. Rosanvallon, *Le Sacre du citoyen*; Helen Cam, *The Hundred and the Hundred Rolls: An Outline of Local Government in Medieval England* (London: Methuen, 1930); C. McIlwain, *Constitutionalism and the Changing World: Collected Papers* (London: Cambridge University Press, 1939); McIlwain, *Growth of Political Thought in the West*; G. Jacobson, *Apple of Gold: Constitutionalism in Israel and the United States* (Princeton, N.J.: Princeton University Press, 1993).

12. K. M. Baker, *The French Revolution and the Creation of Modern Political Culture* (Oxford: Pergamon Press, 1987).

13. J. Schmidt, "Civil Society and Social Things: Setting the Boundaries of the Social Sciences," *Social Research* 62, no. 4 (1995): 899–932; J. Cohen and A. Arato, *Civil Society and Political Theory* (MIT Press, 1992); V. Perez Diaz, *The Return of Civil Society: The Emergence of Democratic Spain* (Cambridge, Mass.: Harvard University Press, 1993).

CHAPTER 4

1. Toulmin, *Cosmopolis*.

2. D. Outram, *The Enlightenment* (Cambridge: Cambridge University Press, 1995); Salomon, *In Praise of Enlightenment*; Salomon, *Tyranny of Progress*.

3. M. Lilla, *Making of an Anti-Modern* (Cambridge, Mass.: Harvard University Press, 1993); Lilla, "Was Ist Gegenaufklarung?" *Merkur* 566 (1966): 400–411; I. Berlin, "Two Concepts of Liberty," in *Four Essays on Liberty* (London: Oxford University Press, 1975), 118–72; Berlin, *Vico and Herder* (New York: Hogarth Press, 1976); Berlin, *Against the Current* (New York: Hogarth Press, 1980); Berlin, *The Crooked Timber of Humanity* (New York: J. Murray, 1991); G. Vico, *The New Science of Giambattista Vico*, abridged and rev. ed. (Garden City, N.Y.: Anchor Books, 1961); J. Herder, *J. G. Herder on Social and Political Culture* (Cambridge: Cambridge University Press, 1969).

4. Toulmin, *Cosmopolis*; J. Habermas, *The Philosophical Discourse of Modernity* (Cambridge, Mass.: MIT Press, 1987); H. Blumenberg, *Die Legitimat der Neuzeit* (Frankfurt: Suhrkamp, 1987); S. N. Eisenstadt, ed., *Post-Traditional Societies* (New York: Norton, 1972); Taylor, *Hegel and the Modern Society*; Taylor, *Sources of the Self: The Making of the Modern Identity* (Cambridge, Mass.: Harvard University Press, 1989).

5. See, in greater detail, S. N. Eisenstadt, *Power, Trust and Meaning* (Chicago: University of Chicago Press, 1995), esp. chap. 3.

6. N. Elias, *The Court Society* (Oxford: B. Blackwell, 1983); Elias, *The Civilizing Process* (New York: Urizen Books, 1978–82); M. Foucault, *The Birth of the Clinic: An Archaeology of Medical Perception* (New York: Vintage Books, 1973); Foucault, *Technologies of the Self: A Seminar with Michel Foucault* (Amherst, Mass.: University of Massachusetts Press, 1988); Foucault, *Surveiller et punir: Naissance de la prison* (Paris: Gallimard, 1975); Foucault, *Madness and Civilization: A History of Insanity in the Age of Reason* (New York: Pantheon Books, 1965).

7. C. Castoriadis, *Philosophy, Politics, Autonomy* (Oxford: Oxford University Press, 1991), esp. chaps. 7 and 8.

8. M. Weber, *Die Protestantische Ethik: Kritiken und Antikritiken* (Guetersloh, Germany: Guetersloher Verlagshaus, 1978); Weber, *Politik als Beruf* (Berlin: Dunker and Humblot, 1968); Weber, *On Charisma and Institution Building: Selected Papers* (Chicago: University of Chicago Press, 1968); Weber, *The Rational and Social Foundations of Music* (Carbondale, Ill.: Southern Illinois University Press, 1958); W. G. Runciman, ed., *Max Weber: Selections in Translation* (Cambridge: Cambridge University Press, 1978).

9. P. Wagner, *A Sociology of Modernity: Liberty and Discipline* (London: Routledge, 1994).

10. Z. Sternhell, ed., *The Intellectual Revolt against Liberal Democracy, 1870–1945* (Jerusalem: Israel Academy of Sciences and Humanities, 1996); S. Holmes, *The Anatomy of Antiliberalism* (Cambridge, Mass.: Harvard University Press, 1993).

See, for instance, F. W. Nietzsche, *On the Genealogy of Morality* (Cambridge: Cambridge University Press, 1994); Nietzsche, *The Will to Power* (New York: Vintage Books, 1967); Nietzsche, *Beyond Good and Evil* (Chicago: Gateway, 1955); Nietzsche, *The Living Thoughts of Nietzsche* (London: Cassell, 1942). For a good selection, see W. Kaufmann, ed., *The Portable Nietzsche: Selected and Translated* (New York: Viking Press, 1965). See also S. Aschheim, "Nietzsche and the German Radical Right, 1914–1933," in Sternhell, ed. *Intellectual Revolt against Liberal Democracy*, 159–76.

E. Jünger, *Feuer und Blut* (Magdeburg: Stahlhelm Verlag, 1925); Jünger, *Der Kampf also inneres Erlebnis* (Berlin: Mittler, 1929); Jünger, "Der Arbeiter," in his *Werke*, vol. 6 (Stuttgart: E. Klett, 1964).

M. Heidegger, *Hegel's Phenomenology of Spirit* (Bloomington, Ind.: Indiana University Press, 1988); Heidegger, *The Fundamental Concepts of Metaphysics* (Bloomington, Ind.: Indiana University Press, 1995); Heidegger, *German Existentialism* (New York: Philosophical Library, 1965); One of the best works on Heidegger is G. Steiner, *Martin Heidegger* (New York: Viking Press, 1979).

11. J. Herf, "Reactionary Modernism Reconsidered: Modernity, the West and the Nazis," in Sternhell, ed., *Intellectual Revolt against Liberal Democracy*, 131–58; J. Muller, "The Radical Conservative Critique of Liberal Democracy in Weimar Germany: Hans Freyer and Carl Schmitt," in ibid., 190–218.

Jünger, *Feuer und Blut*; Jünger, *Der Kampf also inneres Erlebnis*; Jünger; Jünger, "Der Arbeiter."

H. Freyer, *Theorie des Objektiven Geistes: Eine Einleitung in die Kulturphilosophie* (Leipzig: B. G. Teubner, 1923); Freyer, *Die Industriegesellschaft in Ost und West: Konvergenzen und Divergenzen* (Mainz: V. Hase and Koehler, 1966).

C. Schmitt, *Politische Theologie: Vier Kapitel zur Lehre von der Souveraenitaet* (Munich: Duncker and Humbolt, 1922); Schmitt, *Political Romanticism* (Cambridge, Mass.: MIT Press, 1986); Schmitt, *Die Diktatur: Von den Anfaengen des Modernen Souveraenitaetsgedankens bis zum Proletarischen Klassenkampf* (Berlin: Duncker and Humbolt, 1989); Schmitt, *The Concept of the Political* (New Brunswick, N.J.: Rutgers University Press, 1976); Schmitt, *The Crisis of Parliamentary Democracy* (Cambridge, Mass.: MIT Press, 1988).

12. Lilla, "Was Ist Gegenaufklarung?"

13. See, for instance, S. A. Kierkegaard, *Two Ages: The Age of Revolution and the Present Age* (Princeton, N.J.: Princeton University Press, 1977); Kierkegaard, *Fear and Trembling and the Sickness unto Death* (Princeton, N.J.: Princeton University Press, 1974).

Nietzsche, *On the Genealogy of Morality*; Nietzsche, *Will to Power*; Nietzsche, *Beyond Good and Evil*; Nietzsche, *Living Thoughts of Nietzsche*; Kaufmann, ed., *Portable Nietzsche*. See also Aschheim, "Nietzsche and the German Radical Right."

A. Schopenhauer, *On the Basis of Morality* (Providence, R.I.: Berghahn Books, 1995); Schopenhauer, *The World as Will and Representation* (New York: Dover Publications, 1966); Schopenhauer, *Essay on the Freedom of the Will* (Indianapolis: Bobbs-Merrill, 1960).

L. Strauss, *The Rebirth of Classical Political Rationalism: An Introduction to the Thought of Leo Strauss* (Chicago: University of Chicago Press, 1989); Strauss, *The*

Political Thought of Hobbes: Its Basis and Its Genesis (Chicago: University of Chicago Press, 1973).

14. Voegelin, *Enlightenment and Revolution*; Voegelin, *New Science of Politics*; Voegelin, *Die Politischen Religionen*; Voegelin, *Das Volk Gottes*.

15. L. Kolakowski, *Modernity on Endless Trial* (Chicago: University of Chicago Press, 1990).

CHAPTER 5

1. C. Lefort, *Democracy and Political Theory* (Minneapolis: University of Minnesota Press, 1988). See also Arnason, "Theory of Modernity and the Problematic of Democracy"; J. Dryzek, "Political Inclusion and the Dynamics of Democratization," *American Political Science Review* 90, no. 3 (1996): 475–87; J. Dunn, *The History of Political Theory and Other Essays* (Cambridge: Cambridge University Press, 1996).

2. J. Nedelski, *Private Property and the Limits of American Constitutionalism* (Chicago: University of Chicago Press, 1990).

3. J. Rousseau, *The Social Contract and Discourses*, ed. and introd. G.D.H. Cole (New York: Dutton Everyman's Library, 1968).

4. J. Dunn, *Locke* (Oxford: Oxford University Press, 1984); Dunn, *Rethinking Modern Political Theory* (Cambridge: Cambridge University Press, 1978), esp. pt. 1.

5. J. Keane, ed., *Civil Society and the State: New European Perspectives* (London: Verso, 1988); Oakeshott, *Social and Political Doctrines of Contemporary Europe* (London: Basis Books, 1940).

6. Talmon, *Origins of Totalitarian Democracy*. See also Arnason, "Theory of Modernity and the Problematic of Democracy"; Leforte, *Democracy and Political Theory*, 57–163; *Totalitarian Democracy and After: International Colloquium in Memory of Jacob L. Talmon*, 37–56.

7. N. Bobbio, *Il Futuro della Democrazzia* (Torino: Giulio Einaudi Editore, 1984); Bobbio, "Postfazione," in Bobbio, *Profilo Ideologico del Novecento Italiano* (Torino: Giulio Einaudi, 1986), 177–85; Bobbio, *L'eta dei diritti* (Torino: G. Einaudi, 1990); N. Matteucci, "Democrazia e autocrazia nel pensiero di Norberto Bobbio," in *Per una teoria generale della politica: Scritti dedicatti Norberto Bobbio* (Florence: Passignli Editori, 1983), 149–79.

8. On the Jacobin elements in modern polities, see A. Cochin, *La Revolution et la libre pensee* (Paris: Plon-Nourrit, 1924); Cochin, *L'esprit du Jacobinisme* (Paris: Universitaires de France, 1979); J. Baechler, preface in ibid., 7–33; F. Furet, *Rethinking the French Revolution* (Chicago: University of Chicago Press, 1981); Talmon, *Origins of Totalitarian Democracy*. See also J. L. Salvadori and N. Tranfaghia, eds., *Il Modelo politico giacobino e le rivoluzione* (Florence: La Nova Italia, 1984); M. Salvador, *Europe, America, Marxismo* (Torino: Einaudi, 1990), chap. 7., E. Frankel,

"Strukturdefekte der demokratie und deren unberwindung" and "Ratenmythos und soziale selbstbestimmung." in Frankel, ed., *Deutschland und die Westlichen Demokratien* (Frankfurt am Main: Suhrkamp, 1990), 68–95 and 95–137, respectively.

A very strong statement against the emphasis on "common will" in the name of "emancipation" can be found in H. Luebe, *Freiheit statt Amanzipationszwang: Die Liberalen Traditionen und das Ende der Marxistischen Illusionen* (Zurich: Edition Interfrom, 1991).

9. Eisenstadt, "Transcendental Vision, Center Formation, and the Role of Intellectuals."

10. Fontana, ed., *Invention of the Modern Republic.*

11. Lubbe, *Freiheit statt Amanzipationszwang;* Berlin, "Two Concepts of Liberty."

12. Shils, "Primordial, Personal, Sacred, and Civil Ties."

CHAPTER 6

1. Cam, *Hundred and the Hundred Rolls;* McIlwain, *Constitutionalism;* McIlwain, *Growth of Political Thought in the West.*

2. On the Great Revolutions and their background, see Eisenstadt, *Revolutions and the Transformation of Societies;* Eisenstadt, "Historical Sociology Revolutions," *International Social Science Journal* 133 (1992): 386–401; M. Lasky, "The Birth of a Metaphor: On the Origins of Utopia and Revolution," *Encounter* 34, no. 2 (1970): 35–45, and no. 3 (1970): 30–42; Lasky, *Utopia and Revolution* (Chicago: University of Chicago Press, 1976).

On the Great Revolutions and modernity, see for instance the special issue on "The French Revolution and the Birth of Modernity," *Social Research* 56, no. 1 (1989).

On the role of groups of heterodox intellectuals in some of the revolutions and in the antecedent periods, see A. Cochin, *La Revolution et la libre pense;* Cochin, *L'esprit du Jacobinisme;* J. Baechler, preface in ibid., 7–33; F. Furet, *Rethinking the French Revolution;* V. C. Nahirny, *The Russian Intelligentsia: From Torment to Silence* (New Brunswick, N.J.: Rutgers, Transaction Publication, 1981).

3. Edward Shils, "The Virtue of Civil Society," *Government and Opposition* 26 no. 1 (Winter 1993): 11. See J. Keane, "Introduction," 1–31, and "Despotism and Democracy," 35–72, both in Keane, ed., *Civil Society and the State.*

4. P. Schmitter and T. Karl, "What Democracy Is . . . And Is Not," *Journal of Democracy* 2 no. 3 (1991): 76–78.

5. Eisenstadt, *Modernization: Protest and Change.* See also Ch. Bright and Hardings, eds., *State Making and Social Movements* (Ann Arbor, Mich.: University of Michigan Press, 1984); R. Burton, *Dissent and Reform in the Early Middle Ages* (Berkeley, Calif.: University of California Press, 1965).

6. A. Pizzorno, *Le radici della politica assoluta* (Milano: Giangiacomo Feltrinelli Editore, 1994).

7. See C. S. Maier, ed., *Changing Boundaries of the Political* (Cambridge: Cambridge University Press, 1987); A. Przeworski, *Capitalism and Social Democracy* (Cambridge: Cambridge University Press, 1985).

8. B. Ackerman, *We the People* (Cambridge, Mass.: Harvard University Press, 1991); S. N. Eisenstadt, "Barbarism and Modernity," *Society* 33, no. 4 (1996): 31–38; Lasky, "Birth of a Metaphor"; Lasky, *Utopia and Revolution.*

9. For general analysis of social movements, see S. Tarrow, *Power in Movement: Social Movements, Collective Action and Politics* (Cambridge: Cambridge University Press, 1994); Pizzorno, *Le radici della politica assoluta*; H. Bash, *Social Problems and Social Movements: An Exploration into the Sociological Construction of Alternative Realities* (Atlantic Highlands, N.J.: Humanity Press, 1995); A. Morris and C. McClurg Mueller, eds., *Frontiers in Social Movement Theory* (New Haven, Conn.: Yale University Press, 1992); P. Snowden, *Socialism and Syndicalism* (London: Collins' Clear-Type Press, 1953); G. Sorel, *Reflections on Violence* (New York: Collier Books, 1961); Sorel, *Materiaux d'une theorie du proletariat* (New York: Arno Press, 1975); W. Elliot, *The Pragmatic Revolt in Politics: Syndicalism, Fascism and the Constitutional State* (New York: H. Fertig, 1968); J. Joll, *The Anarchists* (London: Eyre and Spottiswoode, 1964).

For the history of different movements in selected societies, see; In Asian countries: J. Mathew, *Ideology, Protest and Social Mobility: Case Study of Mahars and Pulayas* (New Dehli: Inter-India, 1986); B. Kesavanarayana, *Political and Social Factors in Andhra (1900–1956)* (Vijayawada: Navodaya, 1976); D. Apter, *Revolutionary Discourse in Mao's Republic* (Cambridge, Mass.: Harvard University Press, 1994); G. Bennett, *'Yundong' Mass Campaigns in Chinese Communist Leadership* (Berkeley, Calif.: University of California Press, 1976); E. Koury, *The Patterns of Mass Movements in Arab Revolutionary-Progressive States* (The Hague: Mouton, 1970); C. Uyehara, *Left-Wing Social Movements in Japan: An Annotated Bibliography Published for the Fletcher School of Law and Diplomacy* (Tokyo: Tufts University and C. E. Tuttle, 1959).

In Latin America: D. La Botz, *Democracy in Mexico: Peasant Rebellion and Political Reform* (Boston: South End Press, 1995); W. Assies, *To Get Out of the Mud: Neighborhood Associativism in Recife, 1964–1988* (Amsterdam: Cedla, 1992); C. Schneider, *Shantytown Protest in Pinochet's Chile* (Philadelphia: Temple State University Press, 1995); S. Stokes, *Cultures in Conflict: Social Movements and the State in Peru* (Berkeley, Calif.: University of California Press, 1995).

In Western Europe: D. Della Porta, *Social Movements, Political Violence and the State: A Comparative Analysis of Italy and Germany* (Cambridge: Cambridge University Press, 1995); S. Sarkar, *Green-Alternative Politics in West Germany* (New Dehli: Promilla and Co., 1993); C. Boggs, *Social Movements and Political Power: Emerging Forms of Radicalism in the West* (Philadelphia: Temple University Press, 1986).

In Eastern Europe: C. Joppke, *East German Dissidents and the Revolution of 1989: Social Movements in a Leninist Regime* (New York: New York University Press,

1995); K. Opps, *Origins of a Spontaneous Revolution, East Germany, 1989* (Ann Arbor, Mich.: University of Michigan Press, 1995); V. Brovkin, *Behind the Front Lines of the Civil War: Political Parties and Social Movements in Russia, 1918–1922* (Princeton, N.J.: Princeton University Press, 1994); V. Kostunica, *Party Pluralism or Monism: Social Movements and the Political System in Yugoslavia, 1944–1949* (Boulder, Colo.: East European Monographs, 1985).

In North America: D. Steigerwald, *The Sixties and the End of Modern America* (New York: St. Martin's Press, 1995); R. Jackson, *The 1960s: An Annotated Bibliography of Social and Political Movements in the United States* (Westport, Conn.: Greenwood Press, 1992); B. Berry, *America's Utopian Experiments: Communal Havens from Long-Wave Crisis* (Hanover, N.H.: University Press of New England, 1992); T. Reed, *Fifteen Jugglers, Five Believers: Literary Politics and the Poetics of American Social Movements* (Berkeley, Calif.: University of California Press, 1992); E. Morgan, *The 60s Experience: Hard Lessons about Modern America* (Philadelphia: Temple University Press, 1991); R. Goldberg, *Grassroots Resistance: Social Movements in Twentieth Century America* (Belmont, Calif.: Wadsworth, 1991).

10. On the new social movements, see S. Aronowitz, *The Politics of Identity: Class, Culture, Social Movements* (New York: Routledge, 1992); K. Karst, *Law's Promise, Law's Expression: Visions of Power in the Politics of Race, Gender and Religion* (New Haven, Conn.: Yale University Press, 1993); O. Banks, *Faces of Feminism: A Study of Feminism as a Social Movement* (Oxford: Martin Robertson and Company, 1981); G. West and R. Blumberg, eds., *Women and Social Protest* (New York: Oxford University Press, 1990); E. Jelin, ed., *Women and Social Change in Latin America* (Geneva: United Nations Research Institute for Social Development, 1990); Pizzorno, *Le radici della politica assoluta.*

CHAPTER 7

1. Tilly, *Coercion, Capital, and European States.*

2. S. N. Eisenstadt, *Jewish Civilization: The Jewish Historical Experience in a Comparative Perspective* (New York: State University of New York Press, 1992), esp. chap. 4; Eisenstadt, *The Transformation of Israeli Society* (London: Weidenfeld & Nicolson, 1985); M. Shalev, "The Political Economy of Labor-Party Dominance and Decline in Israel," in T. Pempel, ed., *Uncommon Democracies: The One-Party Dominant Regimes* (Ithaca, N.Y.: Cornell University Press, 1990), 83–127; D. Horowitz and M. Lissak, *Trouble in Utopia: The Overburdened Polity of Israel* (New York: State University of New York Press, 1989).

3. Gloria Goodwin Raheja, "India: Caste, Kingship, and Dominance Reconsidered," *Annual Review of Anthropology* 17 (1988): 517; L. Dumont, *Homo Hierarchicus: The Caste System and Its Implications* (Chicago and London: University of

Chicago Press, 1980); A. Beteille, *Caste, Class, and Power: Changing Patterns of Stratification in a Tanjore Village* (Berkeley, Calif.: University of California Press, 1965); K. Ishwaran, ed., *Change and Continuity in India's Villages* (New York: Columbia University Press, 1970); D. G. Mandelbaum, *Society in India*, 2 vols. (Berkeley, Calif.: University of California Press, 1970).

4. A. Seligman, "The Failure of Socialism in the United States: A Reconsideration," in S. N. Eisenstadt, L. Roniger, and A. Seligman, eds., *Centre Formation: Protest Movements and Class Structure in Europe and the United States* (London: Frances Pinter, 1987), 90–119; D. Bell, "The Background and the Development of Marxian Socialism in the United States," in D. Egbert and S. Persons, eds., *Socialism and American Life* (Princeton, N.J.: Princeton University Press, 1952).

5. G. Rozman, "Edo's Importance in the Changing Tokugawa Society," *Journal of Japanese Studies*, 1, no. 1 (1974): 91–112; D. Howell, "Ainu Ethnicity and the Boundaries of the Early Modern Japanese State," *Past and Present*, no. 142 (1994): 69–93; M. B. Jansen, "State and Society in Tokugawa Japan," (paper presented at the symposium "State and Society in East Asia," Paris, May 1991); Jansen, *Japan and Its World* (Princeton, N.J.: Princeton University Press, 1980).

6. Horowitz and Lissak, *Trouble in Utopia.*

7. R.J.Z. Werblowsky, *Beyond Tradition and Modernity* (London; Athlone Press, 1976). See also C. Blacker, "Two Shinto Myths: The Golden Age and the Chosen People," in S. Kenny and J. P. Lehman, *Themes and Theories in Modern Japanese History* (London: Athlone Press, 1988), 64–78; Downing, "Constitutionalism, Warfare, and Political Change in Early Modern Europe."

8. M. Waida, "Buddhism and the National Community," in F. E. Reynolds and T. M. Ludwig, eds., *Transitions and Transformations in the History of Religions* (Leiden: Brill, 1980), 221–41. See also Blacker, "Two Shinto Myths"; Werblowski, *Beyond Tradition and Modernity.*

9. P. Nosco, *Confucianism and Tokugawa Culture* (Princeton, N.J.: Princeton University Press, 1984).

10. P. Duus, "Bounded Democracy: Tradition and Politics in Modern Japan," unpublished.

11. R. N. Bellah, "Civil Religion in America," *Daedalus* 96, no. 1 (Winter 1967): 1–21; Bellah, *The Broken Covenant* (New York: Seabury Press, 1975); J. Laslett and S. M Lipset, eds., *Failure of a Dream: Essays in the History of American Society* (New York: Anchor Books, 1974).

12. W. F. Naylor, "Some Thoughts upon Reading Toqueville's *Democracy in America*" (paper presented at Professor Edward Shils's seminar on "Ideas on Social Solidarity," University of Chicago, May 1995).

13. I owe this observation to Tom Burns.

14. S. P. Huntington, *American Politics: The Promise of Disharmony* (Cambridge, Mass.: Harvard University Press, 1981).

CHAPTER 8

1. A. Przeworski, "Democracy as a Contingent Outcome of Conflicts," in J. Elster and R. Slagstad, eds., *Constitutionalism and Democracy* (Cambridge: Cambridge University Press, 1989), 59–81; Przeworski, "Some Problems in the Study of the Transition to Democracy," in O'Donnell, Schmitter, and Whitehead, eds., *Transitions from Authoritarian Rule: Comparative Perspectives*, 47–53.

2. A. Przeworski, *Capitalism and Social Democracy* (Cambridge: Cambridge University Press, 1985).

3. O'Donnell, Schmitter and Whitehead, eds., *Transitions from Authoritarian Rule: Comparative Perspectives*; O'Donnell and Schmitter, *Transitions from Authoritarian Rule: Tentative Conclusions about Uncertain Democracies*; Linz and Stepan, *Problems of Democratic Transition and Consolidation*; Diamond, ed., *Political Culture and Democracy in Developing Countries*; Diamond, Linz, and Lipset, eds., *Democracy in Developing Countries*; Diamond, Linz, and Lipset, eds., *Politics in Developing Countries*.

4. Claus Offe, "Trust and Knowledge, Rules and Decisions: Exploring a Difficult Conceptual Terrain" (paper presented at the conference "Democracy and Trust," Georgetown University, Washington, D.C., November 7–9, 1996), 3–4.

5. Ibid., 3.

6. See, in greater detail, Eisenstadt, *Power, Trust and Meaning*.

7. S. M. Lipset and S. Rokkan, eds., *Party System and Voter Alignments* (New York: Free Press, 1967); S. Rokkan, "Dimensions of State Formation and Nation Building: A Possible Paradigm for Research on Variations Within Europe," in C. Tilly, ed., *The Formation of National States in Western Europe* (Princeton, N.J.: Princeton University Press, 1975), 562–600.

8. E. Huber, D. Ryeschmeyer, and J. D. Stephans, "The Paradoxes of Contemporary Democracy: Formal, Participatory, and Social Democracy," *Comparative Politics*, 29, no. 3 (1997): 323–43.

9. See, in greater detail, S. N. Eisenstadt, *The Protestant Ethic and Modernisation: A Comparative View* (New York: Basic Books, 1968).

10. Eisenstadt, *Jewish Civilization*; Eisenstadt, *European Civilization in a Comparative Perspective* (Oslo: Norwegian University Press, 1987); S. Rokkan, "Dimensions of State Formation and Nation Building: A Possible Paradigm for Research on Variations within Europe," P. Birnbaum and I. Katznelson, eds., *Paths of Emamcipation: Jews, States and Citizenship* (Princeton, N.J.: Princeton University Press, 1995).

11. Eisenstadt, "Barbarism and Modernity."

12. B. Hagtvet, "The Theory of Mass Society and the Collapse of the Weimar Republic: A Re-Examination," in S. U. Larsen, B. Hagtvet, and J. P. Myklebust, eds., *Who Were the Fascists? Social Roots of European Fascism* (Bergen: Universitetsforlaget, 1981), 66–118.

13. Ibid., 461-62.

14. E. Lindström, *Fascism in Scandinavia, 1920-1940* (Stockholm: Liber, 1985).

15. Ibid.; S. Graubard, ed., *Norden: The Passion for Equality* (Oslo: Norwegian University Press, 1987); Stein Kuhnle, *Patterns of Social and Political Mobilization: A Historical Analysis of the Nordic Countries* (Beverly Hills, Calif.: Sage Publications, 1975).

16. See, on this, S. N. Eisenstadt, *Japanese Civilization: A Comparative View* (Chicago: University of Chicago Press, 1996).

17. Bellah, "Civil Religion in America." See also Bellah, *Broken Covenant*; Laslett and Lipset, eds., *Failure of a Dream.*

18. G. De Meur and D. Berg-Schlosser, "Conditions of Authoritarianism, Fascism, and Democracy in Interwar Europe: Systematic Matching and Constrasting of Cases for 'Small N' Analysis," *Comparative Political Studies* 29, no. 4 (1996): 423-68.

19. See M. Burton, R. Gunther, and J. Highley, "Elites and Democratic Consolidation—Latin America and Southern Europe: An Overview," in J. Highley and R. Gunther, eds., *Elites and Democratic Consolidation in Latin America and Southern Europe* (Cambridge: Cambridge University Press, 1992), 323-348.

CHAPTER 9

1. S. Huntington, M. Crozier and J. Watanuki, *The Crisis of Democracy* (New York: New York University Press, 1975).

2. W. Kymlicka, *Multicultural Citizenship: A Liberal Theory of Minority Rights* (Oxford: Clarendon Press, 1995).

3. On the nation-state, see G. Eley and R. G. Suny, eds., *Becoming National: A Reader* (New York: Oxford University Press, 1996), esp. 403-508. See also the issue on "Nationalism Reexaminded," *Social Research* 63, no. 1 (1996).

4. Weber, *Die Protestantische Ethik;* Weber, *Antikritiken;* Politik als Beruf; Weber, *On Charisma and Institution Building;* Weber, *Rational and Social Foundations of Music;* Runciman, ed., *Max Weber: Selections in Translation;* Elias, *Court Society;* Elias, *Civilizing Process;* Foucault, *Birth of the Clinic;* Foucault, *Technologies of the Self;* Foucault, *Seminar with Michel Foucault;* Foucault, *Surveiller et punir;* Foucault, *Madness and Civilization.*

5. "Some Observations on 'Post-Modern' Society," in Volker Bornschier, et. al., eds., *Diskontinuitat des Sozialen wandels* (Frankfurt: Campus Verlag: 1990), 287-96.

6. Eisenstadt and Giesen, "Construction of Collective Identity"; Shils, "Primordial, Personal, Sacred, and Civil Ties."

7. L. Diamond, "Introduction: In Search of Consolidation," in Diamond, M. Plattner, Yun-han Chu, and Hung-mao Tien, *Consolidating the Third Wave De-*

mocracies: Regional Challenges (Baltimore: Johns Hopkins University Press, 1997), xiii–1; L. Diamond, M. Plattner, Yun-han Chu, and Hung-mao Tien, *Consolidating the Third Wave Democracies: Themes and Perspectives* (Baltimore: Johns Hopkins University Press, 1997); L. Diamond, "Conclusion: Causes and Effects," in Diamond, ed., *Political Culture and Democracy in Developing Countries*, 411–36; Linz and Stepan, *Problems of Democratic Transition and Consolidation*.

8. R. Dahrendorf, *The Modern Social Conflict: An Essay on the Politics of Liberty* (Berkeley, Calif.: University of California Press, 1990).

9. E. Huber, D. Rueschmeyer, and J. D. Stephens, "The Paradoxes of Contemporary Democracy: Formal, Participatory, and Social Democracy," *Comparative Politics* 29, no. 3 (April 1997): 323–43.

10. R. Kaplan, "Was Democracy Just a Moment?" *Atlantic Monthly* 280, no. 6 (1997): 55–75; Fareed Zakaria, "The Rise of Illiberal Democracies," *Foreign Affairs* 76, no. 6 (1997): 22–43; Zakaria, "Constitutional Liberals Ought to Be the Goal," *New York Herald Tribune*, December 8, 1997, 8. See also Stephen S. Rosenfelder, "Liberal Democracy Is about More Than Voting," ibid.

INDEX